Understanding Gender and Early Childhood

Understanding Gender and Early Childhood is a comprehensive and accessible introduction into the main issues around gender and what these mean for our youngest children. Drawing on key theories and research, and illustrating each topic with case studies, reflective questions and a summary of key points, students are encouraged to question why it is more relevant than ever to consider gender issues and to reflect critically on their own practice and on the practice of others.

The three parts examine gender in relation to the children, the workforce and wider society, concluding with inclusive suggestions for the future of the early years classroom. Topics covered include:

- how gender impacts on children's play, learning and achievement,
- the gender imbalance in the early years workforce and the impact of this on children,
- the gendered ways in which people engage with children,
- gender issues in children's health.

This book is an essential read for those studying on Early Years and Early Childhood courses, along with practitioners and anyone else who wants to develop their understanding of the most pressing issues relating to gender and early childhood practice.

Jo Josephidou is a Lecturer in Early Childhood at the Open University, UK.

Polly Bolshaw is a Senior Lecturer in Early Childhood Studies at Canterbury Christ Church University, UK.

Understanding Gender and Early Childhood

An Introduction to the Key Debates

Jo Josephidou and
Polly Bolshaw

LONDON AND NEW YORK

First edition published 2020
by Routledge
2 Park Square, Milton Park, Abingdon, Oxon, OX14 4RN

and by Routledge
52 Vanderbilt Avenue, New York, NY 10017

Routledge is an imprint of the Taylor & Francis Group, an informa business

© 2020 Jo Josephidou and Polly Bolshaw

The right of Jo Josephidou and Polly Bolshaw to be identified as authors of this work has been asserted by them in accordance with sections 77 and 78 of the Copyright, Designs and Patents Act 1988.

All rights reserved. No part of this book may be reprinted or reproduced or utilised in any form or by any electronic, mechanical, or other means, now known or hereafter invented, including photocopying and recording, or in any information storage or retrieval system, without permission in writing from the publishers.

Trademark notice: Product or corporate names may be trademarks or registered trademarks, and are used only for identification and explanation without intent to infringe.

British Library Cataloguing-in-Publication Data
A catalogue record for this book is available from the British Library

Library of Congress Cataloging-in-Publication Data
A catalog record has been requested for this book

ISBN: 978-0-367-14017-5 (hbk)
ISBN: 978-0-367-14018-2 (pbk)
ISBN: 978-0-429-02977-6 (ebk)

Typeset in Palatino
by Swales & Willis Ltd, Exeter, Devon, UK

To all our boys

Contents

List of Illustrations — viii

1 Introduction: Still talking about gender? — 1

Part I A gendered child — 17

2 Does a child's gender impact on how they play? — 19

3 Does a child's gender impact on how they learn? — 32

4 Does a child's gender impact on how they achieve? — 46

Part II A gendered workforce — 59

5 Why is there a gender imbalance in the early years workforce? — 61

6 What is the impact of the gender imbalance in the early years workforce? — 73

7 How can we achieve a more gender-balanced workforce? — 87

Part III A gendered society — 103

8 Is caring gendered? — 105

9 Motherhood and fatherhood: Do parents engage with their children in gendered ways? — 119

10 Gender issues in health: Are there any differences? — 134

Part IV Conclusion — 151

11 Ways forward: How can we disrupt gendered scripts in the Early Years? — 153

Index — 166

Illustrations

Tables

1.1	Labels used to talk about sex and gender in non-binary, non-essentialist ways (adapted from Zevallos, 2014)	3
1.2	Key ideas around post-structuralism (informed by Paechter, 2001)	5
1.3	How one employer asks prospective employees to identify their gender and sexual orientation	7
4.1	Taking responsibility for tackling gender inequalities	51
6.1	Showing children's perspectives on the gender imbalance in the ECEC workforce	81
6.2	Debating whether more men are needed in the early years workforce	83
8.1	Defining professional love	111
9.1	Linking anecdotal evidence about parents to literature	123
9.2	Considering the argument for and against tailoring practitioner guidance based on parental gender	125
10.1	Identifying features of effective gender-sensitive approaches	143
10.2	Connell's (2005) Framework of Masculinities (adapted from Josephidou, 2017)	144
11.1	Getting your audience to think about gender	160

Figure

5.1	'Thinking-about-gender' continuum (adapted from Connell, 2016)	66

CHAPTER

1

Introduction

Still talking about gender?

Introduction

It's 2019; everywhere we look we can see female leaders, powerful women, enjoying success like never before. Our (predominantly female) students tell us that they can do anything they want to in life, that they are not hampered by their gender and that it is purely personality that determines what their opportunities will be. In the same breath, they recount stories of being followed home in the dark, men unable to keep their hands to themselves in public spaces and how differently their brother is treated by their parents. *We* have decided to keep talking about gender and believe that if you are going to work with young children and impact positively on their lives, then you should be talking about it too. In this first chapter we will:

- build your understanding of what is meant by the term 'gender' using key theoretical lenses,
- explore some of the reasons why it is important to consider gender issues in the context of early childhood,
- highlight the structure of the book and how the chapters are linked and build on each other.

We will consider how, despite major advances in gender equality over the last 50 years, it continues to be important to examine the impact of gender issues in the UK and beyond (Girlguiding, 2018; UN Women, 2017) particularly if we work with young children and their families. We will explore how gender issues at a macro level shape early childhood and, conversely, how what happens in the early years impacts on how society moves forward in relation to gender. We will consider the problematic nature of talking about gender (Ashley, 2003; Rohrmann and Brody, 2015) and define what we mean by the term 'gender' as a social construction, in contrast to the biological label of 'sex'. We will set out the feminist, post-structuralist approach of the book, which Robinson and Jones Diaz (2006) assert can be helpful in challenging 'normalising discourses that operate on micro and macro levels' (p. 17). At the same time, we will explore some of the difficulties in adopting a binary approach for this kind of discussion (Butler, 1990). We will briefly introduce some key theoretical thinkers on gender who can help us understand the gendered discourses (Burn and Pratt-Adams, 2015) and gendered behaviours we may observe in the early years workplace.

What do we mean by the term gender?

The minute we use the word 'gender' we open a whole can of worms. What do we actually mean? We can draw on theoretical models to look for definitions but what does gender mean to the person in the street, to the parents of the children some of you work with in the early years setting, or your colleagues and fellow students who work alongside you? It may seem like a simple term but like many simple terms it is highly contentious and open to debate. In this section of the chapter we will set out the definitions of gender we will use in this book; at the same time, we recognise its problematic nature. We will also highlight some of the key writers on gender who have helped us arrive at these definitions.

The problematic nature of talking about gender

Often conversations about gender can turn into arguments, or we can begin to contradict ourselves, going around in circles but never really getting anywhere or resolving anything. One reason for this difficulty is because gender is not an unchangeable truth written in stone; rather, it is a concept constructed in very many ways influenced by the individual who defines it and everything that has impacted on the formation of their identity. If we throw into this confused mix the way that society has conflated sex with gender, then we can see how difficult it is as a concept to define and talk about.

We are sure that in your day-to-day conversations you will have discovered that talking about gender is problematic. The minute we begin to use the terms male and female we start to get into trouble. First, we need to define what being male and female means. Next, we need to take into account the context in terms of geography and period of history. In addition to this, the impact of class, ethnic background, education and religion on gender definitions must be considered. There are so many ways of doing and performing gender (Butler, 1990) that if we take what is called an essentialist or binary approach (man/woman, boy/girl, male/female) this is really not helpful. One of the issues with looking at gender this way, which has traditionally been the case and still dominates our narratives, is that a process of 'othering' occurs; as Ashley (2003) asserts, 'masculinity must be defined in opposition to femininity' (p. 258). But what if this is an artificial othering? What if there are more differences, for example, between different males than there are between males and females? What does gender mean anyway?

Gender is often defined as a social construct; that is, it is seen as something which is not an absolute truth that exists but rather as an understanding of how people choose, or are obliged, to act in specific, gendered ways. Connell and Pearse define it as 'the way human society deals with human bodies and their continuity, and the many consequences of that "deal" in our personal lives and our collective fate' (2015). Importantly, they reference the physical body here in their definition because this is how we as a society generally make assumptions about the gender, or sex, of our fellow humans.

When we talk about a person's sex, however, we have a very different understanding to when we talk about their gender. Sex is a biological term which suggests a fixed, essentialist and physiological attribute of an individual. It brings with it assumptions about the role of '"natural" differences between men and women' (Rohrmann and Brody, 2015, p. 407). A further confusion arises when society equates gender and sex, assuming a natural alignment between them. Table 1.1 demonstrates how we can never assume this is the case, and sets out some of the more diverse ways we can talk about sex and gender. At the same time as acknowledging these labels, we must also recognise their dynamic nature and that the ways people identify are not set in stone; one person could adopt several of these labels in a lifetime.

TABLE 1.1 Labels used to talk about sex and gender in non-binary, non-essentialist ways (adapted from Zevallos, 2014)

Label	Definition
Sex	A person's biological category, based on chromosomes, hormones and genitalia.
Gender	Culturally constructed categories about who a person is, usually based on sex and also associated with behaviour and personality traits.
Cis-gender	When the gender someone was assigned at birth aligns with their gender identity.
Transgender	When a person's gender identity does not align with the gender identity they were assigned at birth.
Intersexuality	When an individual has ambiguous genitalia, chromosomes or hormones.
Gender queer	When an individual draws on several gender positions or does not identify with a specific gender.
Non-binary	When an individual does not identify with a specific gender.
Gender fluid	When an individual has a changing gender identity, not one fixed identity.
Agender	When an individual rejects gender categories.
Third gender	A term used to describe an established additional gender category in certain cultures.
Heterosexual	When an individual is sexually attracted to people of the opposite sex or gender.
Homosexual	When an individual is sexually attracted to people of the same sex or gender.
Gay	When an individual is homosexual (usually defines a man).
Lesbian	A homosexual woman.

(continued)

TABLE 1.1 *(continued)*

Label	Definition
Bisexual	When an individual is sexually attracted to both men and women.
Pansexual	When an individual is sexually attracted to people of any sex or gender (often used interchangeably with bisexual).
Asexual	When individuals do not feel sexual attraction.

We can see from all these terms and definitions that it is no simple matter to talk about gender; before we discuss gender we need to define it, we need to situate it and we need to be clear how we are linking it to the concept of sex. All the while we must be aware of our own assumptions, beliefs and values.

Theoretical lenses to help us think about gender

If we think about gender only in a common-sense, anecdotal way this will not help us get very far or indeed solve any issues that arise around gender. As in all other areas of our work with young children and their families, we need to draw on theoretical ideas to help us understand what might be happening and indeed challenge and disrupt taken-for-granted practices which we feel should not be happening. With this in mind, in this chapter we will set out the feminist, post-structuralist approach of the book which Robinson and Jones Diaz (2006) assert can be helpful in challenging 'normalising discourses that operate on micro and macro levels' (p. 17).

It was the rise of feminism that helped society acknowledge that gender relations were a key area that needed to be explored. In particular, it is post-structuralist feminism that explores 'issues of knowledge, power, difference, and discourse and how these intersect and entwine in the lives of women' (English, 2012, p. 2). If we think about the early years workforce, for example, we are talking predominantly about women (approx. 97% according to recent figures by the Department for Education (2019)); this fact should make us consider questions around why this is so and what the impact could be; questions we will explore throughout this book. Therefore, theoretical ideas around post-structuralism and feminism are an appropriate and useful lens to help us consider some answers. The term 'feminism' has now become part of our everyday speech, even if there is often disagreement about its meaning. There are many different definitions of feminism and indeed many different forms of feminism, so before we go any further, we will consider how we are going to use the term in this book. We will use the term 'feminism' to describe a way of thinking, seeing and doing that challenges, disrupts and rejects some common and traditional ways of talking about what it means to be a man or woman; these ways are influenced by the traditional structures of patriarchy. So, what ideas do we mean? It might be helpful if we state some of them here:

- Looking after children, or a home, is not 'real work'.
- Caring jobs, outside the home, do not need to be well-paid.
- Women need to become more like men to have equal status in society.
- Male and female are binary opposites and therefore two homogeneous groups.
- Some kinds of knowledge are seen as more important than others.
- Feminine and masculine traits are innate.

We agree with Richards' suggestion that 'men and women are under different social pressures, encouraged to do different kinds of work, behave differently, and develop different characteristics' (1982, p. 155).

We have also used the adjective 'post-structuralist' to inform our thinking about feminism so let us now consider this term and consider how it could support us in our practice when working with young children.

Post-structuralism is a prevalent theoretical lens, with many interpretations, which has helped us to understand gender relations in a different way. We have to confess, like Mukherji and Albon (2009, p. 31) that this is not at all a simple theory while at the same time borrowing their simple explanation that it is a theory that 'problematises the idea that the "truth" is knowable', often seeking to disrupt that which is *seen* to be true. Paechter (2001) gives a useful overview of post-structuralist ideas and how they can support a more nuanced understanding of gender. If you look at Table 1.2 below, you will see we have set out some of the key concepts involved in post-structuralism, defined them and then given an example of how concepts might align to early years practice.

TABLE 1.2 Key ideas around post-structuralism (informed by Paechter, 2001)

Key Concept	Definition	Links to Early Years
The concept of discourse	'A discourse is a way of speaking, thinking or writing that presents particular relationships as self-evidently true' (p. 1).	When we say in the early years setting that 'boys need to play outside more' or 'girls prefer drawing more than boys'.
Power and resistance are inseparable	'Human agency ... to [deconstruct] ... discourses and ... [construct] ... resistant counter-discourses' (p. 5).	When we take small steps to challenge the above discourses that have become normalised then we contribute to disrupting harmful gendered patterns.
Metanarratives are to be distrusted	'... metanarratives [such as capitalism, patriarchy, etc. which] tell big, explanatory stories about the world as a whole ... privilege ways of thinking and behaving' (p. 6).	If we subscribe to child-centred narratives as part of our pedagogy, we may not think it is appropriate to challenge children if they are engaged in ways of being that reinforce gender.

(continued)

Introduction

TABLE 1.2 *(continued)*

Key Concept	Definition	Links to Early Years
Emotion can help us understand our world	What we feel is as important (if not more important) than our ability to reason and think logically about the world.	A key example here is the often acknowledged 'passion' of the early years practitioner which drives her to work tirelessly for little pay to impact on outcomes for young children. Yet because she is in a 'caring' role this is viewed by society as low status; see in particular Chapter 8 (Is caring gendered?).

We can use these ideas, which Paechter acknowledges are drawn from Foucault (1980), to help us challenge the 'normalising discourses' (Robinson and Jones Diaz, 2006, p. 17) we will often come across in the world of Early Years, whether as a student, practitioner or parent.

But what does 'challenging normalising discourses' actually mean in practice? The term 'discourse' comes from Foucault, a French philosopher whose work focussed on power, gender and inequalities. Others have used the term 'scripts' (as in gender scripts by Burn and Pratt-Adams (2015)) or narratives. Foucault defined discourses as 'practices that systematically form the objects of which they speak' (2002, p. 54). So we could say that, in his view, by talking about things we make them real; for example by talking about gender differences we make them real. Therefore, we need to disrupt these discourses by challenging them if we want to move forward in terms of gender equality.

Binary approaches

One of the ways we have traditionally talked about gender, particularly in the West, is by using the male/female binary; this means that when describing children you have to make a choice over one or the other. Birth certificates ascribe a gender label based on the perceived sex of a newborn baby; we say 'perceived' because it is not always a clear-cut case to identify which genitalia a baby has been born with and therefore which sex, and consequently gender, they should be ascribed.

There has been a growing awareness that subscribing to one of two genders, male or female, is problematic in many ways. Official forms, especially in the UK context, have moved away from asking people to choose from two essentialist positions but there is still much confusion. Organisations need to ask questions about the gender of their job applicants to ensure they are meeting the stipulations of the Equality Act (2010); however, this is done in various ways – not all of them without problems. For example, a recent (2019) application form for a professional position asked the applicant to respond to the following questions in Table 1.3.

TABLE 1.3 How one employer asks prospective employees to identify their gender and sexual orientation

Please select one of each of the following sections that best describes you					
Gender					
Male			Female		
Sexual Orientation (Please describe your sexual orientation)					
Towards people of a different sex (straight)	Towards men of the same sex (gay)	Towards women of the same sex (lesbian)	Towards people of both sexes (bisexual)	Other (e.g. asexual)	I prefer not to say

Although there is some recognition here of the difficulties in adopting a binary approach, prospective employees are still asked to choose between male and female to ensure that the employer is being compliant as far as legislation is concerned.

One of the key writers on the problematic nature of binary approaches is Judith Butler. She is a philosopher whose seminal work, *Gender Trouble* (1990), has influenced thinking about gender as a social construction. She ponders the idea that 'gender is the cultural meanings that the sexed body assumes' (p. 9) and as such becomes a 'free-floating artifice' (ibid.); therefore, it is impossible to think in a binary way about males and females. Furthermore, Morgenroth and Ryan (2018, p. 1) suggest that the title *Gender Trouble* (1990) is not necessarily a declaration that thinking about gender is troubling but rather that Butler is encouraging 'society to create "gender trouble" by disrupting the binary view of sex, gender, and sexuality'.

Butler is also seen as a proponent of 'queer theory'. Queer theory can be defined as 'the notion that identities are not fixed or stable, but rather are shifting, contradictory, dynamic and constructed' (Robinson and Jones Diaz, 2016, p. 20). As such we can see that this definition aligns perfectly with an understanding that gender is not fixed but is, rather, something that is performed (Butler, 1990). This reinforces our argument that gender cannot be binary and therefore it is problematic to discuss it as such. Unfortunately, we will contradict ourselves throughout the book and therefore hope the reader will forgive us; we are left with the categories of male/female, boy/girl, men/women, mums/dads to discuss such things as children's attainment, parenting styles and the gendered workforce. As such we could be said to be contributing to the reinforcement of gendered stereotypes, so we hope that the reader will engage with a critical eye in considering any assertions we make.

We have seen how difficult it can be to think in binary ways about gender. Not only does it confuse us, but it is also a particularly ethnocentric way of considering humans. It is good to see, even in the Western context though, that there has been more of a movement in recent years to allow people to label themselves in a greater variety of ways to best align with their identity.

Time to consider

Think about the essentialist ways you may inadvertently think about gender. For example, think about your own gender and then consider what assumptions you have about what you can or cannot do or be. When we talk with students, two things often stand out to us when they talk about gender; firstly, our predominantly female students discuss the fact that they would much rather work with men because all women working together can be 'bitchy' (their term, certainly not ours!), secondly, when they look back on their primary school experiences, they remember fondly their male teachers and how they were, in general, much more 'fun' and 'exciting' than their female teachers. Of course, this observation is only anecdotal and not research-based; however, we have been surprised at how often these discussions have occurred without us prompting them. What do you think? Can you relate to these discussions about males and females and where these ideas come from? What other ideas about gender do you or your peers hold?

Why is it important to consider gender issues in the context of early childhood?

As those who work with young children, we can have a profound effect on both their outcomes and those of their families. We can help them think more creatively by using pedagogies that challenge certain assumptions about gender and also disrupt certain scripts or discourses that both children and adults can use. By so doing, we are subscribing to a pedagogy that both promotes social justice (Solehuddin and Adriany, 2017) and is sustainable. We could say, then, that giving thoughtful consideration to gender issues in the early years is all part of the role of being a reflective practitioner.

Gender equality, young children and their families

It's true that there have been major advances in terms of gender equality over the past 50 years. Some people consider that true equality between men and women has been achieved; after all we have the legislation (Equality Act, 2010) to inform people's actions in the public sphere and women have many more opportunities than they have ever had. Some people even suggest that the pendulum has swung too far and that masculinity is now in crisis. However, if we look at some up-to-date documentation, we will discover that despite these major advances, there are still issues of equality for women wherever we look.

It is important that we look beyond the context of our own situation to get a clear understanding of progress made in terms of gender equality. Sometimes, if our situation is positive, and we do not feel discriminated against because of our gender, we can imagine that others live in similar contexts and have similar opportunities. This is what Connell (2011) believes is part of a neoliberal discourse which asserts that people will talk about 'personality' and 'choice' to explain variations in behaviours and opportunities rather than focus on gender (p. 37). The United Nations takes a world view on gender and looks beyond these individual contexts. It charts the progress of equality for women in its ongoing report 'Progress of the world's women' (UN Women 2017) by looking at data from across the globe. In this report it stated that 'It is clear: the global economy is not working for women' and reiterated women's rights in terms of '… a good job, with equal pay and safe working conditions; the right to an adequate pension; the right to healthcare, and water and sanitation'. Other documentation also highlights that all is not rosy for women in terms of gender equality and how this is linked to their experiences as children.

One such useful resource for finding out what young girls in the UK believe is happening, in terms of gender equality, is the Girls' Attitudes Survey. This is a survey commissioned each year by the Girl Guiding Association and carried out by Childwise. The girls targeted as participants (aged 7–21) do not necessarily belong to the association but are recruited through educational institutions and asked to complete an online survey and/or interview. The 2018 survey of 1903 girls revealed some thought-provoking findings such as:

> … older girls' positivity towards technology and ICT has fallen. The turn-off among 11 to 16-year-olds could be to do with stereotypical views that it's a subject for boys – in our report last year, 30% of girls aged 11 to 16 thought this. The continuing lack of visible female role models in the tech sector and its external profile could also be having an impact.
>
> (Girlguiding, 2018, p. 7)

The authors of the report suggest this is surprising, as the younger age group are showing much more positivity towards technology and ICT; this makes us question what is happening if there is a growing realisation for many girls that this is not an area for them.

Some would suggest that as children grow they 'internalise' the fact that they are limited to two different roles in life; they understand that there are one of two ways to behave: either in the role of a male or the role of a female. This way of looking at gender has been called 'sex role theory'. Connell (2005) would argue, however, that this is not a useful way to theorise if we are trying to understand what happens in gender interactions. She states that it is only:

> … apt for situations where (a) there are well-defined scripts to perform, (b) there are clear audiences to perform to and (c), the stakes are not too high … None of these conditions, as a rule, apply to gender relations … (One can, of course, think of specific situations in gender interactions where roles are definitely played… Ballroom dancing competitions spring to mind …).
>
> (Connell, 2005, p. 26)

This is a really helpful illustration which clearly sets out the difference between highly structured scenarios of gender performance and the everyday interactions of gender that are much more dynamic, nuanced and informed by many, many factors.

We can see then that, as people working with young children, their families and their communities, we need to be aware of gender situations going on in the wider world. We can become so focussed on the context and minutiae of our own lives that we forget to question the gendered implications of our practices at a more macro level. We may work with young children, but we need to question what opportunities they will have, what career trajectories they will be set upon and what the links are between this and our own practice with them while they are still young. We will discuss this more in Chapter 6 (What is the impact of the gender imbalance in the early years workforce?).

Thinking about gender at different levels

Connell (2016) encourages us to think about gender at different levels. We can consider her ideas as a continuum for thinking and talking about gender; at one end are global issues such as femicide and militarisation; at the other, everyday issues of 'intimate relationships, [and] personal identities' (p. 4). Our book, by seeking to explore gender issues in the early years, places itself on this continuum; it recognises that what happens at one end of the 'gender thinking continuum' can impact on what happens at the other.

But is that really true? Can we honestly say that what happens at the global level affects me in my everyday life as a woman or a man? Going back to Connell (2016), we can see that she would suggest that, yes, this is the case. She encourages us to look at what is happening on the world's stage where the key actors are men who bring a specific form of masculinity which is aggressive, unkind and marginalising of women:

> After generations of feminist struggle, men with varying forms of privilege still greatly predominate in positions of global power, in some sectors holding a complete monopoly ... Not just a power-oriented masculinity but also a cultivated callousness is involved in organizing abductions of girls, suicide bombings, femicide, beheadings, and mass addiction. It seems close to the callousness involved in drone strikes, mass sackings, structural adjustment programmes, nuclear armaments, and the relentless destruction of our common environment. Mahatma Gandhi was once asked for his opinion of Western civilization. He replied, 'It would be a good idea'.
>
> (2016, pp. 12–13)

Clearly such an ideology as this will trickle down and impact on what happens in our everyday lives; we could then argue that it would also impact on what happens in the early years setting. But what about influence travelling the other way? Is it realistic to expect that what happens in the early years setting could actually impact on what happens at a global level?

The impact of the early years

We will argue throughout the book that what happens in early years will indeed impact on wider society. We know as practitioners that we can have a profound impact on outcomes for young children – not just by working with them, but in our work with parents and the community beyond the setting. As you read this book, we would like you to position yourself as a 'disrupter' and as one who can speak out and challenge overworn, gendered scripts, practices and behaviours, particularly as far as our interactions with young children are concerned.

We believe that despite the major advances in terms of equality between men and women, boys and girls, we can take nothing for granted in terms of gender equality. Our espoused (what we say) practices are not always enacted (what we do) and lip service can sometimes be felt to be enough. Gender issues on a more macro level can be said to influence gender practices on a more micro level and vice versa. This is why we must continue to talk about gender issues specifically in the early years – already a highly gendered environment because of its predominantly female workforce – and to disrupt those practices, languages and behaviours which support a reinforcing of stereotypes and essentialist approaches to gender.

Time to consider

Take some time to consider some of the gender narratives used in society today. Look at two different sources: one from the mainstream media and one from the professional early years literature; what are people saying about gender? Think about what is being said explicitly but also what is being said between the lines.

What are the themes and objectives of this book?

There are so many assumptions and taken-for-granted practices concerning gender in early childhood. This book is a provocation for all those who work with, or are intending to work with, young children. We want to inspire you to question your own and others' practices as we encourage you to engage with key theories and research about gender which will substantially develop your subject knowledge. Because our writing is underpinned by feminist ideas around pedagogy, we will also ask you to explore gender critically by questioning your own practices and your own 'life histories' (Hogan, 2012).

Introduction

The book is structured around three key themes:

1. gender issues concerning young children (Part I: A gendered child),
2. gender issues concerning the early years workforce (Part II: A gendered workforce),
3. gender issues in wider society which impact on both children and the early years workforce (Part III: A gendered society).

Use the theorists we present to you as critical friends as you journey through this book. Let them challenge you, irritate you and shape your thinking as you engage with ideas about gender in the early years. Some thinkers will resonate much more with you than others; choose the ones that are meaningful to you and will help you develop your thinking. Some difficulty can arise when we begin to think in a theoretical way without considering how this relates to practice, so always look at the practice and then consider how that particular theory may help you to understand it. One of the ways we will help you do this is by introducing a case study in each chapter. The case study is based on something we have observed in practice and we will ask you to reflect on it using some of the theoretical lenses introduced. Never lose sight of the fact that it is seldom helpful to look at gender in isolation, but we must also consider all other factors that can intersect with it and so impact on the individual.

Time to consider

Consider your own gendered identity and how you arrived at it. Do any of the theoretical lenses we have laid out here help you consider how you have become the 'gendered you'?

Case study

An Early Childhood Studies student on placement in a baby room notices the differences in how practitioners address girls and boys. She overhears comments from practitioners like 'Don't cry, you are a big boy' and 'Don't you look a beautiful girl today!' She notes this in the reflective log she must complete, which she then takes back to her university seminar for discussion. She asks her peers in the seminar group if they think this kind of language matters and, if it does, what she should do. If you were in her seminar group what would you say to her and why?

Possible response

This language does matter if it is giving children the message at a very early age that there are important gender differences. For example, it could be giving boys the message that they are not allowed to show emotions or girls that they will be praised and gain approval if they look pretty. This links with the quotation from Richards which suggests the gendered pressures to 'behave differently, and develop different characteristics' (1982, p. 155). It is also introducing them to binary and essentialist ways of thinking about gender and almost asking them to choose. In this scenario it is difficult for a student to challenge, as she is a 'guest' in the setting, however she could be a 'disrupter' by thinking very carefully about the scripts she will choose to use when a child cries or is showing off their princess dress.

Final reflection

Let's take forward our understanding of gender as we continue through the chapters of the book, always remembering that the 'issues are explosive and tangled, the chances of going astray are good' (Connell, 2011, p. ix). However, just because it is difficult does not mean that we should shy away from discussing it; the topic of gender frames so many of the discussions that take place in and around the world of early childhood that it would be remiss of us to avoid it. There are so many ways of doing and performing gender (Butler, 1990); from the stay-at-home dad to the action hero, from the blond Barbie doll to Shuri (the princess and genius in the film *Black Panther*) so taking an essentialist approach where we say 'this is what men are like' and 'this is what women are like' is really unhelpful. Infuriatingly, however, at times it is impossible to continue the discussion without referencing a binary approach to talk about perceived differences between men and women, boys and girls. So please forgive us in advance!

Key points

- Gender is a complex and contentious concept; considering theoretical lenses can help us debate some of the issues that surround it.
- If we work with young children and their families, it is important that we consider the gender issues that impact on their lives.
- This book considers the links between the gendered child, the gendered workforce and the gendered society.

Further reading

1. Girlguiding (2018) *The Girls' Attitudes Survey*. Available at: www.girlguiding.org.uk/globalassets/docs-and-resources/research-and-campaigns/girls-attitudes-survey-2018.pdf (accessed 18th August 2019).

   This is such an accessible and interesting report which provides an insight into what girls (aged 7–21) in the UK context perceive their opportunities and barriers are.

2. Connell, R. (2005) *Masculinities*. Cambridge: Polity Press.

   As a seminal theorist in the area of gender, Connell has so many interesting publications; it can be difficult to signpost a good starting point. However, this book is a really good introduction to her ideas on gender and how we have to first look at the concept of masculinity in order to consider gender issues.

References

Ashley, M. (2003) 'Primary schoolboys' identity formation and the male role model: An exploration of sexual identity and gender identity in the UK through attachment theory', *Sex Education*, 3(3), pp. 257–270.

Burn, E. and Pratt-Adams, S. (2015) *Men Teaching Children 3–11: Dismantling Gender Barriers*. London: Bloomsbury.

Butler, J. (1990) *Gender Trouble: Feminism and the Subversion of Identity*. London: Routledge.

Connell, R. (2005) *Masculinities*. Cambridge: Polity Press.

Connell, R. (2011) *Confronting Equality: Gender, Knowledge and Global Change*. Cambridge: Polity Press.

Connell, R. (2016) '100 million kalashnikovs: Gendered power on a world scale', *Debate Feminista*, 51, pp. 3–17.

Connell, R. and Pearse, R. (2015) *Gender: In World Perspective (Polity Short Introductions)*. Cambridge: Polity Press.

Department for Education (DfE) (2019) *Providers' Finances: Evidence from the Survey of Childcare and Early Years Providers 2018*. Available at: https://assets.publishing.service.gov.uk/government/uploads/system/uploads/attachment_data/file/795332/Frontier_-_SCEYP_2018_Finance_Report_v2.pdf?_ga=2.251010318.965115367.1566851821-1304015426.1554639087 (accessed: 29th August 2019).

English, L.M. (2012) 'Poststructuralist feminism', in: A.J. Mills, G. Durepos, and E. Wiebe (eds) *Encyclopedia of case study research*. Thousand Oaks: Sage.

Foucault, M. (1980) *Power/Knowledge: Selected Interviews and Other Writings 1972–1977*. Hemel Hempstead, Herts: Harvester Press.

Foucault, M. (2002) *Archaeology of Knowledge (Routledge Classics)*. Oxon: Routledge.

Girlguiding (2018) *The Girls' Attitudes Survey*. Available at: www.girlguiding.org.uk/globalassets/docs-and-resources/research-and-campaigns/girls-attitudes-survey-2018.pdf (accessed: 29th August 2019).

Hogan, V. (2012). *Locating my teaching of gender in early childhood education teacher education within the wider discourse of feminist pedagogy and poststructuralist theory*. Paper presented at the Joint AARE/APERA, Sydney. Available at: http://files.eric.ed.gov/fulltext/ED542504.pdf (accessed: 29th August 2019).

Morgenroth, T. and Ryan, M.K. (2018) 'Gender trouble in social psychology: how can Butler's work inform experimental social psychologists' conceptualization of gender?' *Front. Psychol.*, 9(1320), pp. 1–9.

Mukherji, P. and Albon, D. (2009) *Research Methods in Early Childhood*. London: Sage.

Paechter, C. (2001) 'Using poststructuralist ideas in gender theory and research: investigating gender', *Contemporary Perspectives in Education*, pp. 41–51.

Richards, J.R. (1982) *The Skeptical Feminist: A Philosophical Enquiry*. Harmondsworth: Penguin.

Robinson, K.H. and Jones Diaz, C. (2016) *Diversity and Difference in Childhood: Issues for Theory and Practice*. London: Open University Press.

Rohrmann, T. and Brody, D. (2015) 'Questioning methodologies in research on men in ECEC', *European Early Childhood Research Journal*, 23(3), pp. 405–416.

Solehuddin, M. and Adriany, V. (2017). 'Kindergarten teachers' understanding on social justice: Stories from Indonesia', *SAGE Open*, 7(4) https://doi.org/10.1177/2158244017739340

UN Women (2017) *Progress of the World's Women 2015–2016 Summary: Transforming Economies, Realizing Rights*. Available at: http://progress.unwomen.org/en/2015/pdf/SUMMARY.pdf (accessed: 29th August 2019).

Zevallos, Z. (2014) 'Sociology of gender', *The Other Sociologist*, 28 November.

PART I
A gendered child

CHAPTER

2

Does a child's gender impact on how they play?

Introduction

In this first section of the book we are going to focus on children and, more specifically, 'A gendered child'. What do we mean by this term? It suggests that when we look at children we notice not just their biological sex but also how they are gendered, even at a very young age, by the clothes they are dressed in, the toys they are given to play with and the way adults interact with them. We can specifically see this in operation with young babies; it can be difficult to attribute a specific gender to a young baby unless their adult has given us some markers (such as name or colour of clothing) to help us. In this chapter we are interested in how the gendered child plays. Look all around you in the early years setting and watch the children engaged in play. Do you notice anything in particular? For example, are there any gender issues in the way they play or the way that other adults respond to them? Is it always the boys who get told to remember their 'quiet feet' or often the girls who are complimented on their beautiful drawings? We agree that these are stereotypical images, but we bet that if you asked practitioners or parents, these are the sort of scripts (remember Chapter 1 (Introduction: Still talking about gender?)) that would emerge. The disagreement would probably be around whether these play tendencies are innate or due to socialisation. Think back to your own play choices as a child. Perhaps, for example, you can remember asking for certain toys for Christmas. What was it that influenced these requests? Did you want the same as your friends or did TV advertising impact on your Christmas list? All of these are very important questions that we must ask ourselves if we seek to disrupt harmful stereotypes concerning young children. Therefore, in this second chapter we will encourage you to do this by:

- exploring how some research suggests that there are gender differences in the way young children play,
- building your understanding of how practices and discourses in the early years setting can contribute to children playing in gendered ways – and why this matters,

- reflecting on arguments around the problematic nature of a child-centred curriculum in reinforcing gendered discourses and behaviours.

Some of the ideas we will focus on will be centred on research which suggests that boys and girls may play differently. We will consider whether there is evidence to suggest this is inherent (Baron-Cohen, 2003) or a result of their socialisation thus far. For example, we will look at assertions that young boys need more physical play or young girls are more drawn to imaginative play. We will question whether certain areas of provision are dominated by one gender and, if so, what the implications of this are. Furthermore, we will suggest that some practices and ways of talking about gender in the early years setting may reinforce differences in gender play, arguing that child-centred ideologies may prevent practitioners from challenging gendered discourses (Adriany, 2015).

Do boys and girls play differently?

Whether boys and girls play differently is a contested idea (Meland and Kaltvedt, 2019). Some suggest that there are clear differences and that it is especially boys who are drawn to more gendered ways of playing (Bryan, 2018). A further complex issue is whether this is a result of adult interactions around them, and therefore positive reinforcement of these behaviours, or whether, as Baron-Cohen (2003) would assert, there are brain differences which result in males having 'a tendency to analyse and construct systems while women are inclined to empathise'. As we read this quotation, we may have an image in our mind of a group of boys constructing with blocks and two girls sitting in the role-play area cuddling dollies. But is this really to do with brain differences?

Boys at play

Some research suggests that boys do play differently to girls, although it is disputed whether this is an inherent need or due to the way they are socialised. If the latter argument is true, then those working with young children in the early years setting need to question if and how they contribute to this socialisation. Another complex layer is added to the argument if we ask whether the differences in gendered-play behaviours can be attributed to the issue that girls learn to become more compliant and therefore do not make their play needs known as loudly as boys.

There is a suggestion that boys are more likely than girls to engage in gendered play. For example, Bryan (2018) notes that 'boys often tend to be more actively engaged in the (re)production of gendered play' (2018, p. 309). Bryan draws on earlier research to consider whether this happens because 'teachers tended to praise boys for engaging in stereotypical boy activities' (p. 315). Some of these stereotypical activities could be active play, rough-and-tumble and superhero play. If practitioners and teachers praise boys for engaging in this type of play, then their play behaviours could be reinforced.

It is a common discourse that boys just can't seem to sit still; this discourse is often linked to a discussion of boys' and girls' physical development occurring at different rates. It is thought that boys in particular have play and learning needs that require them to move around because they have 'fidgety' ways (Routen et al., 2018). Conversely, it may be that already by preschool, girls have learned to be more compliant and align their behaviours with what is expected of them in a more formal setting than the home. So, whether the play differences are based on inherent biological needs or whether they are due to ideas around socialisation is a point of contention and great discussion.

One of the most contentious points is around whether there are differences in boys' and girls' brains or physiological differences which would inform the type of play that children engage in. The nature/nurture debate is one that has been going on for many years and is perhaps too simplistic in the context of knowledge we now hold in the present day along with ever-advancing scientific discoveries. Lewicki et al. (2018) advise us to adopt a 'psychobiosocial perspective' to understand children's gendered choices and achievements; they draw on Eagly and Wood's work (2013) to remind us that the two big Ns (nature and nurture) are 'inseparably interwoven'. Therefore, there could be many factors, in addition to gender, which inform how both boys and girls play.

Girls at play

Do you remember in Chapter 1 where we talked about the problems of discussing gender in a binary way? We hope you are going to forgive us now because we have to do exactly that here; we have talked about boys, so now we are going to talk about girls. Do you see the difficulty? However, there is some research literature which focuses on the different ways that girls play.

Some of this literature relates to the fact that girls have more advanced language skills at a younger age than boys. For example, Eriksson et al. (2012) carried out a large-scale study of over 13,783 children to try to identify any gender differences. The children were aged 0–2 years old and spoke one of ten different languages, although none were English-speaking. They found that 'across all languages girls are slightly ahead of boys in early communicative gestures, in productive vocabulary, and in combining words. The difference increased with age'. This research, then, would offer support to the idea that girls play differently to boys because they like to use language more and they have the ability to do so from an earlier age.

One of the areas that language is useful for, of course, is fantasy play and there is some suggestion that girls engage in this more than boys. This view, and its accompanying research, somewhat contradicts other research which asserts that boys engage much more in superhero play; believing you are Spiderman and can walk up skyscrapers or that you can fly like Superman would appear to be the very epitome of fantasy play. However, fantasy-play talk which involves getting inside more complex characters with feelings and emotions, and therefore using spoken language to demonstrate these characteristics, relies on a more advanced use of language and accompanying vocabulary than the 'Whizz! Bang! Kapow!' of, say, the Power Rangers. Jones and Glenn (1991, p. 61) found in their research that 'Girls also engaged in person fantasy play more than boys, whereas boys engaged in more object fantasy play … [and that] There were differences in [the] number of verbalisations in pretend play between boys and girls'. In later research (Carlson and Taylor, 2005, p. 93) however, it was noted that 3-4-year olds demonstrated little difference in word use although it was recognised that girls 'were more likely to create imaginary companions' whereas boys 'were more likely to impersonate … characters'. These are interesting findings if we view them alongside other research which suggests further gender differences in play companions and play objects.

There is some research suggesting that girls particularly enjoy fantasy play that focuses on people and relationships rather than the play objects that boys are drawn to. This research is now quite old (Jones and Glenn, 1991) so it would be good to see whether these findings still stand in the context of the increased commercialisation of childhood in 2019; at the same time, these findings do bring to mind current anecdotal scenes of girls relating to each other as witches, princesses or mummies and boys jumping around with lightsabers and swords! At the same time, we recognise the importance of questioning our own assumptions when we describe what we see in practice; sometimes we might see what we want to see (or think we ought to see) as Lynch (2015) found when questioning practitioners about their perceptions of gender differences in play. For example, do we notice these gendered ways of playing because we bring our own socialised views as a lens? Other research suggests these differences may not actually exist (Jing and Li, 2015).

Further gender issues around play

Perhaps the more important questions we should be asking around gender play differences are to do with whether girls actually need the same play opportunities as boys, such as rough-and-tumble play, but indeed end up missing out because there is a constant narrative around boys' needs in this area. Furthermore, we may be worrying so much about girls dressing up as pink princesses that we may fail to notice that in fact they have superheroes they would like to emulate in their play. When we consider the full range of provision in an early years setting, do all children have full access or can others sometimes see their gender as a barrier which prevents them entering certain areas?

Let us look firstly at the question of rough-and-tumble play; this is the playful wrestling that young children often engage in. Research tells us how important 'rough-and-tumble' play is for them (Bosacki et al., 2015; Tannock, 2008). It enables them to develop many skills such as self-control, self-regulation and spatial awareness (ibid.). As far as adults are concerned it is predominantly males (fathers or practitioners) who see this kind of play in a positive way (ibid.) and engage in it with young children (Lamb and Lewis, 2014); in fact, it 'is reported as an important feature of father–child relationships' (Fletcher et al., 2013, p. 746). We will elaborate further on this in Chapter 6 (What is the impact of the gender imbalance in the early years workforce?). When Meland and Kaltvedt (2019) reviewed the research literature to look at differences between boys and girls in play they found:

> …girls are praised for their clothes, hairstyles, appearance, caring nature and empathic behaviour, while boys are commended for physical size and strength…[and] generally given a greater degree of attention and space to express themselves than girls. Boys are expected to be more active, physical and assertive, while for girls it can be difficult to push these boundaries… Therefore, boys are trained from an early age to take active positions and the opposite applies to girls.
>
> (p. 95)

So, it could be that it is purely that girls are not encouraged to engage in rough-and-tumble play as noticeably as boys.

The same could be true of superhero play. We could be so busy trying to get boys to engage in all areas of learning by referencing superheroes that we forget that this might be appropriate for girls also. Tayler and Price (2016, p. 72) assert that girls do seek out, and benefit from, this kind of play although they approach it in a slightly different way to boys, demonstrating superpowers of 'endurance and kindness rather than strength and physicality'. Once again then, are girls sometimes prevented by their gender from joining in some kinds of play?

If we suggest girls are being prevented from certain kinds of play, however implicitly this is done, we then have to wonder who is doing the preventing. We have already suggested that practitioner attitudes may signpost the sort of things girls feel they are allowed to do (Meland and Kaltvedt, 2019) but could other children also be determining the sort of play that is allowed? If we look at MacNaughton's work on block play (2000), for example, we can see how boys dominated this area of provision. MacNaughton worked with practitioners who had noticed certain behaviours from boys in their settings which were described as 'seek and destroy missions' (p. 114). This was particularly noticeable in the block play area and meant the girls would leave. They also noticed three key issues in this area of provision in terms of the way boys behaved towards girls who wanted to play there. The three behavioural issues were:

1   Boys physically challenged girls who tried to enter the block play area.
2   Some 'brave' girls who managed to enter were then challenged as to why they were there.
3   Some girls were 'allowed to enter' if they followed rules and terms set out by the boys.

If we think of the discussion in Chapter 1 around the links between gendered behaviours at a micro level and then those at a more macro level, then this kind of play is very worrying. Already these young boys were exerting some kind of power they felt they had over the girls. We could say, well this is 20 years ago, things have moved on. Perhaps they have, but these little boys are now young men and we wonder if anyone has ever challenged them in these power behaviours. These little girls are now young women and they will still see barriers in terms of pay and career progression. Furthermore, practitioners recount to us anecdotally that similar behaviours still occur.

We have highlighted in this section of the chapter that there is plenty of 'disrupting' we could and should be doing in the early years setting to ensure that some of the problematic scripts around boys' and girls' play needs are discontinued. We need to look at play for the whole child rather than the gendered child so that each child can develop the skills they need and are not prevented from certain play practices because of their gender.

To conclude this section, we have seen that there are opposing narratives about whether boys and girls play differently. Some suggest, like Baron-Cohen (2003), that there is an inherent element, caused by differences in the male/female brain, which in turn is impacted by levels of testosterone. Others would point to issues of socialisation which can begin at a very early age so that the line between nature and nurture becomes blurred. However, regardless of which side of the debate you position yourself on, it is appropriate to consider whether there are ways of encouraging children to approach play in more gender-neutral, or gender-flexible ways by the provision of more open-ended resources and supportive environments which encourage children to engage in a whole remit of play behaviours unconstrained by their gender.

How can practices and discourses in the early years setting contribute to children playing in gendered ways?

In the early years setting in England, we are very much influenced by the Early Years Foundation Stage Statutory Framework (Department for Education, 2017) in describing a 'unique' child who is free from the constraints of any stereotypical expectations placed upon them. But if we got someone to film our interactions with children over a busy week, we wonder what we would see. We say 'busy' because it is exactly when we have little time to reflect on our actions that our true values show. For example, did you see the BBC film *No More Boys and Girls: Can Our Kids Go Gender Free?* It showed an experiment on adults' perceptions of gender-appropriate toys. Adults were asked to play with babies using a range of available toys; the adult choices were very clearly influenced by what they perceived the gender of the child to be, mostly because of how the babies were dressed. We were not given details about the sample size; however, the findings are said to suggest that those babies perceived to be boys were much more likely to be given toys which developed both their physical confidence and their spatial awareness.

If it is common practice for adults to consider the child's gender when engaging them in play, this begs the question – does it matter and why? Is it such a big deal if girls are offered dolls more than boys, or if boys are offered building blocks more than girls? Kollmayer et al. (2018) suggest that it does matter because of the way that certain toys can develop specific skills. This may, in turn, continue to reinforce gender stereotypes. If no adult is taking responsibility for disrupting these stereotypes, then the potential of the children in question is being limited. This is interesting when we consider that the most recent Girls' Attitude Survey (2018), discussed in Chapter 1, found that when girls (11–21) discussed their aspirations for the future, 67% of them believed they did not have the same opportunities as men. Do these opportunities begin to be kept from them, as they play as babies, through the toys they are offered?

Skilled practitioners need to look to disrupt these practices by offering children a wide range of toys to provide for a variety of play experiences. In this way, they are suggesting possibilities to children which could impact on aspirational choices children make as they get older. Adults also need to consider how children are being targeted as 'consumers-without-agency' who will fulfil gender-specific roles such as the nurturing female and the heroic male. Choosing not to disrupt these gendered scripts contributes to reinforcing those stereotypes which benefit very few in society.

Practitioner talk

Practitioners can choose different ways to talk to children depending on the gender of the child they are talking to (Meland and Kaltvedt, 2019). We need to consider here whether there are ways of talking that are inclusive and non-binary, thus avoiding the reinforcement of essentialist gender stereotypes. We may think we do this already but let us look at what the research says.

At times some practitioners can interact with boys in specific ways. They may give boys more attention, comment on stereotypical masculine characteristics (Aina and Cameron, 2011) or address them using male terminology such as 'you guys' rather than the terms of endearment they save for girls such as 'sweetie' (ibid.). It is an easy trap to fall into for a busy practitioner. If a child comes into the setting and declares 'I'm big and strong' or 'I'm a beautiful princess', echoing what they have heard at home, of course we are going to agree with them but are we not then in danger of reinforcing a stereotypical identity? Might there be other ways to respond that would be equally positive but would avoid this reinforcement?

If boys' strength is commented on, then what do practitioners find to complement in girls? Yes, of course, it has to be their appearance! For example, Aina and Cameron suggest that adults will praise girls for 'their clothing, hairstyles, neatness, and helping behaviours' (p. 13). In other contexts, such as Sweden, practitioners have sought to avoid this by looking very carefully at the language they use with young children in the formal early years setting so that they can avoid it becoming a tool for gender consolidation. In the Swedish context, the preschool curriculum directs practitioners to 'counteract traditional gender patterns and gender roles' (Sandstrom et al., 2013, p. 124). A similar statement in the Early Years Foundation Stage (EYFS) Statutory Framework (2017) would then influence what happened in training the workforce so that future practitioners would be taught how to be aware of their language and use less stereotypical ways of engaging with children. We will come back to this in Chapter 7 (How can we achieve a more gender balanced workforce?).

We should be aware and reflective as practitioners when using language with young children, and consider whether we are relating to them in gendered ways. Do we use different adjectives (lively, noisy, curious) to describe boys' behaviour and female attributes (helpful, kind, caring)? Do we notice the appearance of girls more: the clothes they wear and the way they style their hair?

Practitioner expectations

It is not just the words that practitioners use that are problematic but also their unconscious expectations that are then transmitted to children through body language, behaviours and attitudes. Practitioners need to be mindful of gendered expectations and the negative impact these can have.

There are many studies that suggest that teachers have different expectations of boys and girls. They may believe that boys are better at mathematical-type activities whereas girls will be expected to excel more at language-type activities (Gentrup and Rjosk, 2018). This is certainly borne out by the educational choices children make as they progress through the education system, not just in the UK context but globally (OECD, 2012), and the lack of girls studying physics or boys studying languages. It would be interesting to note whether these expectations extend to the early years teacher/practitioner and the toys they direct children, however inadvertently, towards. But once again we need to ask, 'Does it matter?' Do these expectations impact on how children achieve?

Many studies have looked to see if there is a link between teacher expectation and achievement, but this is not always found (Gentrup and Rjosk, 2018). We do know, however, from studies carried out over many years, that what children actually believe about their ability can impact on their achievements. This is a key idea in child development theory and is called 'self-efficacy' (Pajares, 2002). And where do children's beliefs about themselves some from? Yes, we're back to that idea of socialisation and children learning from very early on what boys and girls are supposed to do.

There is much practitioners can do to develop children's self-efficacy, especially in terms of their opportunities and possibilities regardless of their gender. Zero Tolerance (2013) describe this kind of practice as one that 'raise[s] children who can participate fully in the world' (p. 6). Zero Tolerance resources make direct links between gender equalities in early childhood education and care (ECEC) and gender inequalities among adults (2013). It is a charity set up in the Scottish context to tackle violence against women and, as such, the charity clearly identifies the role that ECEC practitioners have to play in challenging gender-stereotypical scripts used with young children which will impact on their gendered, and often detrimental, behaviours as adults.

We will look much more at gender achievement in Chapter 4 (Does a child's gender impact on how they achieve?) but let's remind ourselves here how important play is in young children's lives; it is their work: both how they learn and how they demonstrate their learning. Let us ensure that their learning through play does not include hidden messages about what they are not allowed to do because of their gender. We have seen in this section that there are practices and discourses that should be challenged if we want to disrupt the influence that they have on reinforcing gender stereotypes. These include reflecting on the language we use with children depending on their gender and considering what gendered expectations we might have of children. Furthermore, not only should we reflect on our own behaviours, but we must also be prepared to challenge others when they draw on these practices and discourses. This may also include challenging young children in our care when child-centred pedagogies support them in reinforcing harmful stereotypes – something we will discuss further in the next section of this chapter.

How can a child-centred curriculum reinforce gendered discourses and behaviours?

When we talk about play in ECEC we often focus on the idea of 'child-centredness' (Adriany, 2015). But the term 'child-centredness' can mean different things depending on the context. For example, Georgeson et al. (2015) argue that it means adopting a democratic or romantic view of children that positions them at the centre of their own world. Others interpret the expression in terms of the developmental appropriateness of the play activities offered (Goouch, 2008). Adriany (2015) suggests that the 'child-centred ideology' has become a 'regime of truth' that is accepted without critique. The consequence of this regime is 'passive' practitioners who allow children's gendered ideas to develop unchecked out of fear of being disrespectful towards the child (pp. 70–82).

Starting with the child

Using children's interests as a starting point for their learning is a key part of early years pedagogy. But what if they have learnt, even before crossing the threshold of the early years setting, that boys and girls have to choose different toys, different colours or different behaviours? In this situation it is important not to be the 'passive practitioner' that Adriany (2015) talks about but rather to adopt the role of 'disrupter' so that we are challenging the schemas children have already built up about 'what is a boy?' and 'what is a girl?'

We are certainly not advocating against a child-centred approach as a means to tackling gender inequalities. Starting with the child (Fisher, 2007) and with the knowledge they have accrued, is always going to be central to our work with young children. However, we do need to be alert and observant to ensure that, by letting children learn by building on their own experiences, they are not 'learning' that they are constrained by their gender. Neither do we want them to learn how to constrain others.

Case study

Georgie notices that the block play in her setting seems to be dominated by boys. She wonders if this is because the girls don't want to play in this area of provision or whether there are other reasons preventing them. She asks you if you consider this to be important and, if you do, what she should do about it.

Possible response

You could suggest to Georgie that she could do some close observation of what is happening in the area of provision and note if the girls are being prevented from joining in either through being physically or verbally challenged by the boys (MacNaughton, 1997). Once she has noted these, she could look to disrupt some of these behaviours. For example, could the children come up with a list of rules and terms together which are inclusive and offer all children the opportunity to use the block play?

Final reflection

This chapter has shown that there is some research suggesting that boys and girls do play differently; however, whether this is inherent behaviour informed by biological differences or through a process of socialisation is a contested argument. What is accepted is that there are practices and discourses that are used in the early years setting which may reinforce these different approaches to play rather than encourage children to explore different play behaviours. Some of these practices will be informed by the child-centred nature of early years curricula so that practitioners may feel unable to disrupt gendered scripts used by the children because they may worry about interfering too much in the children's independent play.

Key points

- From a very early age children are given different toys to play with, depending on their gender, and this may contribute to gendered ways of playing.
- Practitioners need to take time to reflect on the language they are using with young children in case this reinforces gender stereotypes.
- A child-centred curriculum could also allow ideas about gender to be reinforced so it is important to look for ways to disrupt these ideas.

Further reading

1. MacNaughton, G. (1997) 'Who's got the power? Rethinking gender equity strategies in early childhood', *International Journal of Early Years Education*, 5(1), pp. 57–66.

   Read what the practitioners in MacNaughton's research did to try and disrupt some of the gendered play that was taking place in the early years setting.

2. OECD (2012) The ABC of gender equality in education. Available at: www.oecd.org/pisa/keyfindings/pisa-2012-results-gender-eng.pdf (accessed 19th August 2019).

   Have a look at this interesting report by the OECD which, although focussing on teenagers, shows some interesting trends which must make us consider the role of Early Years in providing a firm, ungendered, foundation for children as they begin their journey in the education system.

References

Adriany, V. (2015) 'Gender in pre-school and child-centred ideologies: A story from an Indonesian kindergarten', in: S. Brownhill, J. Warin, and I. Wernersson (eds) *Men, Masculinities and Teaching in Early Childhood Education: International Perspectives on Gender and Care*. London: Routledge.

Aina, O.E. and Cameron, P.A. (2011) 'Why does gender matter? Counteracting stereotypes with young children', *Dimensions of Early Childhood*, 39(3), pp. 11–19.

Baron-Cohen, S. (2003) *The Essential Difference: The Truth about the Male and Female Brain*. New York: Basic books.

Bosacki, S., Woods, H. and Coplan, R. (2015) 'Canadian female and male early childhood educators' perceptions of child aggression and rough-and-tumble play', *Early Child Development and Care*, 185(7), pp. 1134–1147.

Bryan, N. (2018) 'Playing with or like the girls': advancing the performance of 'multiple masculinities in Black boys' childhood play' in U.S. early childhood classrooms', *Gender and Education*, doi:10.1080/09540253.2018.1447091

Carlson, S.M. and Taylor, M. (2005) 'Imaginary companions and impersonated characters: Sex differences in children's fantasy play', *Merrill-Palmer Quarterly*, 51(1), pp. 93–118.

Department for Education (DfE) (2017) Statutory framework for the early years foundation stage. Available at: www.foundationyears.org.uk/files/2017/03/EYFS_STATUTORY_FRAMEWORK_2017.pdf (accessed: 19th August 2019).

Eagly, A.H. and Wood, W. (2013) 'The nature–nurture debates: 25 years of challenges in understanding the psychology of gender', *Perspectives on Psychological Science*, 8(3), pp. 340–357.

Eriksson, M., Marschik, P.B., Tulviste, T., Almgren, M., Perez Pereira, M. and Wehberg, S. (2012) 'Differences between girls and boys in emerging language skills: Evidence from 10 language communities', *British Journal of Developmental Psychology*, 30(2), pp. 326–343.

Fisher, J. (2007) *Starting from the Child*. Maidenhead: Oxford University Press.

Fletcher, R., St. George, J. and Freeman, F. (2013) 'Rough and tumble play quality: Theoretical foundations for a new measure of father–child interaction', *Early Child Development and Care*, 183(6), pp. 746–759.

Gentrup, S. and Rjosk, C. (2018) 'Pygmalion and the gender gap: Do teacher expectations contribute to differences in achievement between boys and girls at the beginning of schooling?' *Educational Research and Evaluation*, 24(3–5), pp. 295–323.

Georgeson, J., Campbell-Barr, V., Bakosi, E., Nemes, M., Pálfi, S. and Sorzio, P. (2015) 'Can we have an international approach to child-centred early childhood practice?', *Early Child Development and Care*, 185(11–12), pp. 1862–1879.

Girlguiding (2018) *The Girls' Attitudes Survey*. Available at: www.girlguiding.org.uk/globalassets/docs-and-resources/research-and-campaigns/girls-attitudes-survey-2018.pdf (accessed: 18th August 2019).

Goouch, K. (2008) 'Understanding playful pedagogies, play narratives and play spaces', *Early Years*, 28(1), pp. 93–102.

Jing, M. and Li, H. (2015) 'Effect of partner's gender on early pretend play: A preliminary study of Singapore Chinese preschoolers', *Early Child Development and Care*, 185(8), pp. 1216–1237.

Jones, A. and Glenn, S.M. (1991) 'Gender differences in pretend play in a primary school group', *Early Child Development and Care*, 77(1), pp. 127–135. doi:10.1080/0300443910770112

Kollmayer, M., Schultes, M., Schober, B., Hodosi, T. and Spiel, C. (2018). Parents' judgments about the desirability of toys for their children: Associations with gender role attitudes, gender-typing of toys, and demographics. *Sex Roles*. Advance online publication. 10.1007/s11199-017-0882-4.

Lamb, M.E. and Lewis, C. (2014) 'Father child relationships', in: N.J. Cabrera and C.S. Tamis-Lemonda (eds) *Handbook of Father Involvement: Multidisciplinary Perspectives*, 2nd edn. Hove: Routledge.

Lewicki, K., Franze, M., Gottschling-Lang, A, and Hoffman, W. (2018) 'Developmental differences between preschool boys and girls in Northeastern Germany', *European Early Childhood Education Research Journal*, 26(3), pp. 316–333. doi:10.1080/1350293X.2018.1462997

Lynch, M. (2015) 'Guys and dolls: a qualitative study of teachers' views of gendered play in kindergarten', *Early Child Development and Care*, 185(5), pp. 679–693.

MacNaughton, G. (2000) *Rethinking Gender in Early Childhood*. London: Sage.

Meland, A.T. and Kaltvedt, E. (2019) 'Tracking gender in kindergarten', *Early Child Development and Care*, 189(1), pp. 94–103.

OECD (2012) The ABC of gender equality in education. Available at: www.oecd.org/pisa/keyfindings/pisa-2012-results-gender-eng.pdf (accessed 19th August 2019).

Pajares, F. (2002) 'Gender and perceived self-efficacy in self-regulated learning', *Theory Into Practice*, 41(2), pp. 116–125.

Routen, A.C., Johnston, J.P., Glazebrook, C. and Sherar, L.B. (2018) 'Teacher perceptions on the delivery and implementation of movement integration strategies: The CLASS PAL (Physically Active Learning) Programme', *International Journal of Educational Research*, 88, pp. 48–59.

Sandström, M., Stier, J. and Sandberg, A. (2013) 'Working with gender pedagogics at 14 Swedish preschools'. *Journal of Early Childhood Research*. 11. 123–132. doi:10.1177/1476718X12466205

Tannock, M. (2008) 'Rough and tumble play: An investigation of the perceptions of educators and young children', *Early Childhood Education Journal*, 35(4), pp. 357–361.

Tayler, K. and Price, D. (2016) *Gender Diversity and Inclusion in Early Years Education*. Abingdon: Routledge.

Zero Tolerance (2013) *Just Like a Child: Challenging Gender Stereotyping in the Early Years. A Guide for Childcare Professionals*. Available at: www.zerotolerance.org.uk/resources/Just-Like-a-Child.pdf (accessed: 29th August 2019).

CHAPTER 3

Does a child's gender impact on how they learn?

Introduction

Do you remember in Chapter 1 (Introduction: Still talking about gender?) where we introduced the idea of scripts, narratives and discourses? We discussed the idea that discourses are 'practices that systematically form the objects of which they speak' (Foucault, 2002, p. 54) and we suggested that by talking about things we make them real. We also remarked that we need to disrupt these discourses by challenging them if we want to move forward in terms of gender equality. Therefore, in this chapter we are going to consider some of the gendered scripts around learning which are both prevalent in the early years setting and then subsequently in the primary and secondary school. You might hear such scripts being used as: 'girls are more ready for formal education than boys' or 'boys like to learn in active ways'. Perhaps there are other scripts that spring to mind as you think about it now? Did you have any gendered scripts directed at you when you were younger and in a formal learning environment such as, 'this activity, subject, sport, behaviour is not for someone of your gender'? In the previous chapter we have looked at formal learning settings for the youngest children and noted the key ideas and conversations around young children's gendered approaches to play. Play is seen as a key pedagogy for young children's learning and development so in this chapter we are going to continue the discussion by exploring perceived gender differences in how children learn. Therefore, in this chapter we will:

- examine some of the discussions around gendered approaches to learning and at the same time consider if there is actually evidence for these arguments and, furthermore, how robust this evidence is,
- consider the idea that gender can become a 'straitjacket' for young children in terms of constraining their learning and, if this is the case, reflect on the age at which children begin to feel this constraint,
- ask you to examine some of the established gender divides in choices of subject at both secondary school exam level and university level and consider how this could link back to practices in early childhood.

As we consider whether there are differences in how young boys and girls learn, recognising at the same time that once again we are adopting a problematic binary approach, we must also reflect on whether different ways of engaging in learning are influenced by biology or society (Bem, 1981; Connell, 2005). It is important that we critique some of the evidence that suggests that boys and girls have different learning styles and consider instead whether other factors may be in place (Crenshaw, 2012). We will also evaluate initiatives which have been introduced to engage boys more in learning, such as football-focused schemes, examining how such programmes have the potential to reinforce gender stereotypes (Anderson, 2012). On the one hand, we argue that gender can be seen as a construct and that any perceived approaches to learning are due to the way that children are socialised; on the other hand we cannot ignore that patterns of similar gendered messages can be seen across different cultural and geographical contexts and that these patterns do impact on the ways that boys and girls are seen to learn (GEAS, 2017).

Do gendered approaches to learning exist?

Go into any early years setting and practitioners will tell you about the differences between boys and girls and how they learn; ask any of the parents dropping their children off and they will no doubt explain the differences they have observed between their sons and daughters. Perhaps you will be told about boys who just can't sit still or girls who like to sit and draw and then help tidy everything up. What we do need to ask ourselves, as people who are both studying and working with young children, is whether these anecdotal differences, which have become embedded in our discussions about young children, are supported by any evidence in research and also how much we have a responsibility to disrupt them through both our words and our actions.

Boys need physical approaches to learning

There is a common discourse that boys need to learn in a much more active, kinaesthetic way. Certainly, this is a discourse that has trickled through continuing professional development (CPD) training for teachers. For example, Burn and Pratt-Adams (2015) cite examples of male teachers and senior managers who have 'attended training sessions about "boys" learning styles … [where] … The focus is firmly on "failing" boys' and how they 'seem to tackle things a lot better through a physical learning approach' (p. 89).

One concern that early years practitioners and teachers often have, as they seek to ensure that children in their care are 'school ready', is the difficulty that many children, and in particular boys, have in sitting still. They notice this at whole-class teaching times such as story time, circle time or even if the children have to attend assemblies. This is an idea that can be reinforced through reading the early childhood literature. For example Ouvry (2003) describes how boys' brains develop differently to girls and that they 'first develop the part of the brain to do with movement and space' (p. 18). She continues to describe how boys are therefore disadvantaged in settings which favour 'sedentary activities which focus on children who can be compliant' (ibid.), which other literature suggests may be because they are female. However, it is not only said that boys find sitting still difficult but also that they may learn much more effectively if they are allowed to be active.

Indeed, there is a common discourse that if boys are allowed to move around then they will be able to learn more, and more quickly. For example, instead of asking them to sit at a table and colour a worksheet on 3-D shapes, it is better to ask them to explore 3-D shapes in the outdoor environment. The only problem with this kind of narrative is that probably many girls would appreciate this approach also as an effective pedagogy, however there is a claim that girls have been socialised to become more compliant and therefore 'put up with' rather than enjoy more superficial ways of learning. Others, such as Ouvry (2003) – although she promotes outdoor, physical engagement for all children regardless of gender – would draw our attention to particular biological differences.

There is also a suggestion, echoing Ovrey's views (2003), that boys' physical development takes a different trajectory to girls. This is an idea we will explore more fully in Chapter 10 (Gender issues in health: are there any differences?) but we will note here that even in the very early days, when children's growth is tracked on growth charts provided by the RCPCH (Royal College of Paediatrics and Child Health), different charts are used for boys and girls as there are different expectations regarding their weight, head circumference, length and height (RCPCH, 2013). Therefore, from the very beginning of their lives there are binary discussions around boys' and girls' physical development. By the time children reach the end of the Early Years Foundation Stage at five years old, girls are outperforming boys, including in the prime area of physical development (Department for Education, 2018).

The way we talk about boys in our settings and schools suggests that they do indeed have very different learning needs, although it is interesting that we don't seem to talk about girls in this way. We roll our eyes in a 'you-know-those-boys' kind of way so that boys become a shorthand for specific needs and attention whereas girls become a byword for compliancy. We discuss boys as those who can't be still and who need to learn in specific ways but do we at the same time forget that girls may have the same or different needs and that, particularly as far as the EYFS (2017) is concerned, we should be looking at the child as unique, regardless of gender?

Gendered interests of young children and their learning

Most teachers and practitioners will tell you how important it is to make a selection of reading material available and in particular to ensure there is enough non-fiction material for 'the boys'. Even though in 2009 the Department for Children, Schools and Families (DfCSF) was advising that this was a myth, nevertheless it is an idea that has prevailed. The suggestion is that boys do not want to be reading stories about fictional characters with feelings and interactions; instead they just want the facts about cars, dinosaurs or football. In fact, Moss and McDonald (2004) suggest that there is very little evidence for this assertion and Paule (2015) terms these scripts as 'dinosaur discourses' which have no place in our consideration of children's learning in 2019. Football in particular has become a key area that it is assumed boys must have an interest in.

Football has often been used in primary schools in a bid to engage boys in learning. For example, the National Literacy Trust has one such initiative which it claims uses the 'appeal of the Premier League and professional football clubs to inspire children to learn, be active and develop important life skills' (National Literacy Trust, 2019). Although this, and other initiatives, never claims to be targeting only boys, and indeed actively state that they want to appeal to boys and girls, they are still problematic because it is argued that football has consistently been used as a tool to reinforce a certain kind of masculinity (Anderson, 2012; Burn and Pratt-Adams, 2015). Football has come to be associated with 'mainstream macho … boys' (Younger et al., 2005, p. 18).

One theory, which can help us understand this adopting of mainstream machoism by boys, is sex role theory (Connell, 2005). Connell describes how we conform to 'a general set of expectations' because of the sex role attached to our gender; we must either behave in a female way or a male way as our masculinity and femininity are purely 'products of social learning'. In some early years settings, there has been an attempt to establish gender-neutral pedagogy in order to prevent these sex roles from being internalised by young children. This can take on many forms such as encouraging children to challenge certain scripts, thinking about layouts that might encourage gendered learning behaviours, not using the terms 'boys' and 'girls' at all, retelling traditional stories that may have a gender bias and encouraging practitioners to constantly reflect on any gendered behaviours they might have in their practice.

To conclude this section of the chapter, we have seen that some research suggests that boys and girls are drawn towards different reading material, although other findings would contest this. Certainly boys' interest in football has been used to try and engage disaffected boys with learning but who is not to say that this would not also engage girls? Either way, the use of football in this manner has been found to be highly problematic (Anderson, 2012; Burn and Pratt-Adams, 2015). Certainly, there is a suggestion, supported by Department for Education data (2018) that boys are slower to pick up certain early skills, but it is important to ask if labelling boys in this manner has biased teacher expectations.

Gender differences in the development of young children's literacy skills

Within global education, girls are often seen to be much better and faster at developing early literacy skills. For example, Solheim and Lundetræ (2018) highlight how boys across a variety of countries, and engaging with a variety of literacy tests, all appear to underachieve compared to girls. However, they go on to question why this gap disappears when the children become adults and ponder on the significance of how these tests are constructed. Furthermore, some of their findings contradict those of Moss and McDonald (2004) by suggesting that boys performed better on information texts than fiction. In the English context, diverse texts are used to assess children's reading in statutory assessments yet still this gender difference in achievement is apparent.

Early years and primary school statutory assessments in the English context would suggest that boys and girls learn in different ways and that perhaps the education system is not giving enough consideration to the different ways that boys learn in order to minimise their apparent underachievement. The most recent Early Years Foundation Stage Profile (EYFSP) (Department for Education, 2018) results show us for example that 77.5% of girls compared to 63.2% of boys achieved expected levels when they were assessed against the Early Learning Goals. Their achievement on this profile can then often be used to place them into ability groups as they transition into Key Stage 1, with boys more often placed in groups titled 'low ability' (Bradbury and Roberts-Holmes, 2017). We could jump to many conclusions as to why this might be the case, and indeed research literature has cited a number of these such as the feminisation of the primary school and the lack of male role models for boys; however the reasons are very complex and it is an issue which cannot be addressed in a superficial way.

Once again then we return to the idea that talking in binary ways about male/female or boy/girl is both problematic and can be unhelpful. We state this because there are many other factors that will impact on children's achievements in the early years, possibly interacting with their gender. This is when it is useful to consider Crenshaw's concept of intersectionality (2012). This concept was not originally introduced to talk about young children; rather, it was an idea that Crenshaw developed to consider the invisibility of African American women within feminist debates. Crenshaw discusses how their experiences are very different and so it is not adequate to look at gender in isolation. In the same way it is useful for us to consider whether the panic about boys' achievement is a panic about all boys or whether it is specific groups of boys who are underachieving. We will return to this discussion in the second section of this chapter.

There is research evidence, such as Department for Education (Department for Education) data and Programme for International Student Assessment (PISA) findings, which suggests that girls do perform much better than boys in early literacy – a key area of development as it impacts on all other areas of learning. For example, if a child cannot read then they cannot read and answer a maths question; if they struggle to write then they cannot show all their knowledge in a mono-modal education system which elevates this way of demonstrating learning above all others. It would be interesting to know whether education systems which value multi-modal ways of evidencing knowledge also show these gender discrepancies. However, it is important to remember that gender achievement is a highly complex issue and that there are many factors besides gender that contribute to explanations of why certain groups of children may underachieve.

To conclude this section of the chapter, there is some suggestion that boys have different learning needs – for example that they need to learn in more physical and active ways and that by targeting their specific learning interests we can support them in really enjoying engaging with learning. There are also suggestions around boys' difficulty with literacy skills. However, other voices would suggest that what works for boys works for all children and the lack of emphasis on girls' learning needs is due to girls learning, through socialisation, to become more compliant.

What other factors interact with children's gender to impact on their approaches to learning?

We noted in the introduction the difficulties in adopting binary arguments about gender. It is far too simplistic to argue 'This is what girls do' or 'This is what boys are like'. Such arguments lead to a labelling of children, a blindness to their potential and a reinforcement of potentially dangerous gender stereotypes. One problem with this kind of essentialist discussion is that it fails to take into account all the many different impacts on a child's disposition to learning. For example, a hungry child, or a child who has no access to books at home, is disadvantaged in learning at school. Whether a child's home learning environment (HLE) values education and cultural impacts will also determine a child's journey through education regardless of their gender. So, if someone ever asserts 'Boys can't sit still' then we need a great deal more information than their gender to understand why sitting still is difficult for them.

The impact of social economic status (SES)

Certainly, there is a perception that a 'certain kind of boy' has different learning needs and abilities in the primary school and so he is grouped accordingly, presumably to 'facilitate' learning. This kind of boy is almost definitely from a perceived lower-class milieu. For example, in Bradbury and Roberts-Holmes' work (2017) they found that the grouping of children into ability sets could be along 'middle class and not middle class groups' (p. 40) and that it was often children 'from disadvantaged backgrounds' who were placed in the 'bottom group' (ibid.). We will explore issues of attainment and achievement in the next chapter, although at this point it is important to highlight the damage that this kind of labelling of children's learning can do.

There is a deficit view of a certain class of child which then transfers into a moral panic about their engagement in learning in the Early Years and the primary school. We are thinking in particular of white working-class boys who are seen to have problems in engaging with teaching in the same way that other children do. They are given a label as a distinct group of learners and then this label not only sorts them, but it sets them on a trajectory of disaffection with education and learning. This situation was very clearly illustrated in a recently released film called *H is for Harry*. This documentary by Mercurial Pictures follows the problematic journey one such boy has within the education system as he struggles to develop literacy skills. Certainly, Harry has difficulties in this area but the struggle of working-class boys as a group to engage in the education system is not only about their intellectual capacity; rather it is about the knowledge, understanding and experiences they take along to school with them in their rucksack along with their lunch boxes and reading folders.

This accumulation of knowledge, understanding and experience was given a theoretical name by Pierre Bourdieu in 1977. He used the term 'cultural capital' to describe how children can be winners or losers in the education system since 'familiarity with the dominant cultural codes in a society, is a key determinant of educational success because it is misperceived by teachers as academic brilliance and rewarded as such' (Jaegera and Mollegaard, 2017, p. 130). Brooker (2015) describes how Bernstein's work (1970) also aligned with this view and furthermore that 'inequalities constructed during early childhood are entrenched during the school years, and persist through the life-course' (Brooker, 2015, p. 34). So, we can see through this argument that it is too simplistic to merely focus on gender when contemplating ways that different groups of children may engage with learning.

We have seen, then, that we cannot consider gender outside the context in which it is being constructed and we must look in particular at how SES may impact on how children are perceived as learners. Certainly, this is a major aspect of the English education system and whereas, at one time in history, academic learning was considered inappropriate for women, it could be argued that it is now considered inappropriate for a certain class of boy. What must be critiqued is how such children, and in particular boys, are viewed in the education system, and also how the knowledge they bring to school is recognised and valued within the education system.

The impact of age on gendered approaches to learning

Some of the seminal child development theorists can support our understanding of how children may learn about gendered behaviours, how they may feel they have to conform to them and how this can impact on the way they learn. For example, developmental theorists such as Piaget (Wray, 1999) could help us understand how the little baby scientist who is constructing their understanding of the world around them quickly begins to engage with ideas such as gender construction and schema using these ideas to adapt their behaviour. Social learning theorists on the other hand help us understand how children then copy gendered behaviour that they see modelled to them (Bandura, 1986).

Kohlberg (1966) believed that children's understanding of gender developed in stages. For example, he notes that in Stage 1 children can identify others as male or female although they do not have an understanding of the permanence of gender. Then as they become older they realise that boys will grow into men and girls into women (Stage 2); it is at this age perhaps that the child begins to relate to gender role models. Finally (Stage 3), when children are about seven years old, they begin to understand that their gender is a stable feature, regardless of how their appearance may change. If Kohlberg was correct in his hypothesis then it seems important that those who work with young children ensure that there are many ways of being male and female beyond those thought to be stereotypical and traditional.

Other child development theories, such as social learning theory (SLT) (Bandura, 1986) suggest that children copy behaviours they see around them and that this could then impact on how they 'learn' their gender. Remember the famous 'Bobo doll' experiment where children copy aggressive behaviour that they see modelled by adults. From this it is very easy to imagine children copying behaviours that they see their peers, older children, familiar adults and celebrities using. We remember, for example, young boys copying the 'spitting' behaviours adopted by professional footballers because they believed that this was an acceptable way for a male who plays football to act. We recall here Anderson's assertion (2012) that football is a key way that the cultural baton of masculinity is passed on. Certainly, by observing these behaviours, young children are building up a schematic understanding of what it is to be a man.

If we think about the idea of schema then of course we are thinking back to the ideas of Piaget and his work on how children construct their understanding of the world around them. In this example then, children would build up a mental shopping list of 'What it means to be a boy' and 'What it means to be a girl' in much the same way as they would build up ideas of what a cat or a dog is. However, in the case of children's understanding of what it means to be a boy or girl, these ideas could become fixed if any gendered misconceptions remained uninterrupted. Gender schema theory developed these ideas when it was introduced by Bem in 1981. Sandra Bem believed that children learnt about gendered roles from the culture they grew up in and that they would consequently learn to adjust their behaviours to ensure they aligned with the cultural norms regarding gender.

To conclude this section of the chapter, child development theory can support our understanding of how children might develop a gendered view on learning and also at what ages this could happen. For example, Piaget and Kohlberg's work can help us to understand how children begin to first label gender and then further understand its consistency. Bandura's observations interweave with this to support an understanding of how children may view behaviours of others around them and then begin to model these behaviours.

Time to consider

Think about the decade when you were a young child. What do you think you put on your 'mental shopping list' of what it means to be a boy or girl? Now think of a child growing up this year. Do you think their shopping list would be the same? How might it have changed?

The impact of culture on gendered approaches to learning

Although there are common patterns surrounding issues around gender globally, as evidenced for example by the Global Early Adolescent Study (GEAS) (2017) or the OECD (2012), there are also issues particular to specific cultures when we consider gender identity and socialisation. Although the last thing we want to do here is to talk in stereotypes, both in terms of culture and gender, it is of interest and useful to look at some evidence which supports an understanding of how gender is transferred from generation to generation within specific cultural contexts. This is an idea that we will also develop in Chapter 6 (What is the impact of the gender imbalance in the early years workforce?)

We have already noted in the previous chapter the context of Sweden ECEC and its curriculum which makes practitioners accountable for challenging gender equality in the setting. We would imagine, then, that this should have a very positive impact and that children would grow up in the Swedish context with a much more flexible approach to the behaviours and scripts they believe they are allowed to adopt. However, Lofdahl and Hjalmarsson (2015) set out clearly the

> 'tensions in the everyday practices of the pre-school between the pre-school teachers' efforts to apply "gender pedagogy" – for example, distributing the toys and tools used in domestic environments such as a dolls corner – and the children's ways of dealing with the implications of these efforts'
>
> (p. 37).

This is a tension mirrored in many other cultures such as, for example, Indonesia.

Similar to the early years provision in many other countries, Indonesia has a child-centred early years curriculum. This means that the practitioner starts with the interests of the child and as such seeks not to dominate but to take a more passive role in allowing the child freedom to explore ideas and concepts through play. Such a curriculum in the Indonesian context has been seen as problematic, though, because teachers can feel unable to disrupt children's gendered practices because of the constraints of a child-centred curriculum. Adriany's (2015) research in this area supports our understanding of gendered approaches to learning and development outside the context of the minority world which has for so long dominated discussions around these issues.

Elsewhere there is research to suggest that some gendered approaches to learning are not consistent across cultures. For example, Akande (1999), when looking at differences in Nigeria, Australia, Hong Kong and South Africa found that the differences depended on the cultural context; therefore, differences claimed through research in the US context were not always evidenced in other cultures. Yet again we are reminded of Crenshaw's ideas around intersectionality (2012) and therefore that we need a much more 'intersectionalist' approach to understand gender interactions (Christensen and Jensen, 2014).

To sum up this discussion of cultural impact, we have seen that even though some cultures (such as Sweden) start to try and disrupt traditional gender norms when children are very young, this is still no easy task. Some of the issues arise from the tensions we discussed in Chapter 2 (Does a child's gender impact on how they play?) surrounding the use of child-centred curricula. However, research drawn from the minority world often points at gendered approaches to learning which are not seen consistently across all cultures.

We have seen, then, that we cannot simply look at gender when we are looking at the different ways that children learn; that would be far too simplistic and is a good example once again of how binary thinking can be unhelpful. We must also ensure we look at other factors that may determine how gender is 'done' by children in the context of the learning environment, whether that is the classroom or the early years setting. These factors could be such things as socio-economic status, or something as simple as age. We must also ensure that we consider how culture could impact on how a child learns regardless of their gender.

What are the links between practices in early childhood and subsequent gendered learning choices made later in life?

Links between learning and gendered career choices

When we look at the many reasons why there is a lack of male practitioners in Early Years (which we will do more fully in Chapter 5 (Why is there a gender imbalance in the early years workforce?)) it would be interesting to know when boys decide to rule themselves out of this kind of work and also if girls rule themselves out from certain careers as well. For example, when do children come to understand the concept of 'women's work'? Michel Foucault uses the concept of 'genealogy' (1972) to explore where our ideas come from. Perhaps part of the genealogy of adolescent career choices comes from actions they have seen their parents carrying out, or the scripts they use.

Certainly, within the English context, when children arrive at 16 years and have to specialise in terms of their subject choices they are going to make those choices informed by how they have been socialised and by their subconscious beliefs about what is appropriate for their gender (their gender schema ideas) (Bem, 1981). They could then be on a gendered conveyor belt that conveys them towards both constrained higher education choices and/or career and job options.

There could therefore be links between what happens in the early years setting and later learning choices – for example, if children believe that certain subjects are not open to them. If some of the gendered scripts around learning are not disrupted, then this could impact on children's trajectories and what they believe they are able to achieve and aspire to later in life. It may dictate the careers they not only believe they have the skills to do but also that they feel they are allowed to do. This is something that is not just seen in the UK or minority world contexts but is something that surveys such as the GEAS (2017) have picked up across cultures and countries.

Case study

Janine is a reception teacher and has been reading about the best way to engage the boys in her class. This is because she has a large group of summer-born boys who sometimes find the more formal aspects of primary school problematic, for example, the requirement for daily phonics. When she implements some of these approaches, she realises that all the children in the class, regardless of their gender, are benefitting. Discuss why you feel this might be the case.

Possible response

Firstly, Janine has realised that this is not just an issue of gender. She has recognised that some children are just not ready for the more formal approaches required by her school. She has sensitively looked at what the children can do and adopted her pedagogy accordingly. It is no wonder that all children are benefitting from such a reflective teacher who has refused to adopt a deficit view of the children but instead looked to change her own practices and behaviours instead of theirs.

Final reflection

Teachers of young children may indeed observe gendered approaches to the way children engage in learning. However, whether these differences are innate or whether this is a result of how the children have been socialised both within the setting and in the home context is something that the reflective practitioner must constantly consider. In this way teachers and practitioners may make changes to their practice that will impact on the learning choices children make as they progress through the education system. The next chapter will go on to consider whether a child's gender impacts on how they achieve when they make these educational choices.

Key points

- Research evidence suggests that boys and girls can have different learning needs, but this could be more an issue of socialisation than inherent need.
- Factors such as age, culture and socio-economic status can also impact on approaches to learning.
- Children may rule themselves out from certain careers if certain gendered scripts are not disrupted when they are young.

Further reading

1. www.hisforharry.com/home

   Have a look at the website for *H is for Harry*; there are some interesting resources to explore alongside some important statistics to consider.

2. Paule, M. (2015) 'Dinosaur discourses: taking stock of gendered learning myths', *Gender and Education*, 27(7), 744–758.

   Read Paule's interesting article about how we need to move on from the 'dinosaur discourses' that describe stereotypical ways that boys and girls learn.

References

Adriany, V. (2015) 'Gender in pre-school and child-centred ideologies: A story from an Indonesian kindergarten', in: S. Brownhill, J. Warin and I. Wernersson (eds) *Men, Masculinities and Teaching in Early Childhood Education: International Perspectives on Gender and Care*. Oxon: Routledge.

Akande, A. (1999) 'Gender differences in approaches to learning: Across cultures', *Early Child Development and Care*, 151(1), pp. 57–76.

Anderson, E. (2012) *Inclusive Masculinity: The Changing Nature of Masculinities*. Oxon: Routledge.

Bandura, A. (1986) *Social Foundations of Thought and Action: A Social Cognitive Theory*. Englewood Cliffs (NJ): Prentice-Hall.

Bem, S.L. (1981) 'Gender schema theory: A cognitive account of sex typing', *Psychological Review*, 88, pp. 354–364.

Bernstein, B. (1970) 'Education cannot compensate for society', *New Society*, 26, pp. 344–351.

Bourdieu, P. (1977) *Reproduction in Education, Society, Culture*. Beverly Hills, CA: Sage.

Bradbury, A. and Roberts-Holmes, G. (2017) *A necessary evil*. Available at: https://neu.org.uk/media/3191/view (accessed: August 29th 2019).

Brooker, L. (2015) 'Cultural capital in the preschool years: Can the state 'compensate' for the Family?' in: L. Alanen, E. Brooker and B. Mayall (eds) *Childhood with Bourdieu*. Hampshire: Palgrave MacMillan.

Burn, E. and Pratt-Adams, S. (2015) *Men Teaching Children 3–11: Dismantling Gender Barriers*. London: Bloomsbury.

Christensen, A. and Jensen, S. (2014) 'Combining hegemonic masculinity and intersectionality', *NORMA: International Journal for Masculinity Studies*, 9(1), pp. 60–75.

Connell, R. (2005) *Masculinities*. 2nd edn. Cambridge: Polity Press.

Crenshaw, K. (2012) *On Intersectionality: Essential Writings*. Jackson, TN: Perseus.

Department for Children, Schools and Families (2009) *Gender and education: Myth busters*. Available at: www.education.gov.uk/publications/eOrderingDownload/00599-2009BKT-EN.pdf (accessed: 20th August 2019).

Department for Education (2017) *Statutory framework for the early years foundation stage*. Available at: www.foundationyears.org.uk/files/2017/03/EYFS_STATUTORY_FRAMEWORK_2017.pdf (accessed: 20th August 2019).

Department for Education (2018) *Early years foundation stage profile results in England, 2018*. Available at: https://assets.publishing.service.gov.uk/government/uploads/system/uploads/attachment_data/file/748814/EYFSP_2018_Main_Text.pdf (accessed: 20th August 2019).

Foucault, M. (1972) *The Archaeology of Knowledge and the Discourse on Language*. New York: Pantheon.

Foucault, M. (2002) *Archaeology of Knowledge (Routledge Classics)*. Oxon: Routledge.

GEAS (2017) *Global early adolescent study*. Available at: www.geastudy.org (accessed: 20 August 2019).

Jaegera, M. and Mollegaard, S. (2017) 'Cultural capital, teacher bias, and educational success: New evidence from monozygotic twins', *Social Science Research*, 65, pp. 130–144.

Kohlberg, L. (1966) 'A cognitive-developmental analysis of children's sex-role concepts and attitudes', in: E. Maccoby (ed) *The Development of Sex Differences*. London: Tavistock.

Lofdahl, A. and Hjalmarsson, M. (2015) ''Children's interpretive reproduction of gender-conscious didactic agendas in a Swedish pre-school', in S. Brownhill, J. Warin and I. Wernersson (eds) *Men, Masculinities and Teaching in Early Childhood Education: International Perspectives on Gender and Care*. Oxon: Routledge.

Moss, G. and McDonald, J.W. (2004) 'The borrowers: Library records as unobtrusive measures of children's reading preferences', *Journal of Research in Reading*, 27(4), pp. 401–413.

National Literacy Trust (2019) *Premier league primary stars*. Available at: https://literacytrust.org.uk/programmes/sport-and-literacy/premier-league-primary-stars/ (accessed: 20th August 2019).

OECD (2012) *The ABC of gender equality in education*. Available at: www.oecd.org/pisa/keyfindings/pisa-2012-results-gender-eng.pdf (accessed: 19th August 2019).

Ouvry, M. (2003) *Exercising Muscles and Minds: Outdoor Play and the Early Years Curriculum*. London: NCB.

Paule, M. (2015) 'Dinosaur discourses: Taking stock of gendered learning myths', *Gender and Education*, 27(7), pp. 744–758.

RCPCH (Royal College of Paediatrics and Child Health) (2013) *UK-WHO growth charts - 0-4 years*. Available at: www.rcpch.ac.uk/resources/uk-who-growth-charts-0-4-years (accessed: 20th August 2019).

Solheim, O.J. and Lundetræ, K. (2018) 'Can test construction account for varying gender differences in international reading achievement tests of children, adolescents and young adults? – A study based on Nordic results in PIRLS, PISA and PIAAC', *Assessment in Education: Principles, Policy & Practice*, 25(1), pp. 107–126.

Wray, D. (1999) 'Teaching literacy: The foundations of good practice', *Education 3–13*, 27(1), pp. 53–59.

Younger, M., Warrington, M., Gray, J., Rudduck, J., Mclellan, R., Bearne, E., Kershner, R. and Bricheno, P. (2005) *Raising boys' achievement*. Available at: www.researchgate.net/publication/242599270_Raising_Boys%27_Achievement (accessed: 20th August 2019).

CHAPTER 4

Does a child's gender impact on how they achieve?

Introduction

Type 'the feminisation of education' into a search engine and you will quickly note a moral panic which has been consistently spreading through the media for the last 20 years. You will see headlines such as:

- 'Tory MP claims boys are disadvantaged by "over-feminised" school system' (*The Independent*, Pells, 2016).
- 'Feminised curriculum "has thrown boy out with bathwater"' (*The Guardian*, Smith, 2006).
- 'The betrayal of our boys' (*The Daily Mail*, Vine, 2016).

Why do we call this a 'moral panic'? This term was introduced in 1972 and then revisited several times (1980, 1987, 2002) by a writer named Stanley Cohen. He used it to describe:

> A condition, episode, person or group of persons ... defined as a threat to societal values and interests; its nature is presented in a stylized and stereotypical fashion ... socially accredited experts pronounce their diagnoses and solutions; ways of coping are evolved or (more often) resorted to; the condition then disappears, submerges or deteriorates and becomes more visible. Sometimes the object of the panic is quite novel and at other times it is something which has been in existence long enough, but suddenly appears in the limelight. Sometimes the panic passes over and is forgotten, except in folklore and collective memory; at other times it has more serious and long-lasting repercussions and might produce such changes as those in legal and social policy or even in the way the society conceives itself.
>
> (Cohen 2002, p. 1)

Certainly, if we consider the headlines above, we can see that there is some kind of panic going on in the media around boys' experience in the education system. Whether this is justified or not is open to debate, both in the research and academic literature and also in practice. In Chapter 3 (Does a child's gender impact on how they learn?) we thought about perceived gender approaches to learning; we will develop the discussion here and consider how gender could impact on a child's achievement. We will question whether it is justified to worry about how boys are doing in the education system. Therefore, in this chapter you will:

- develop your understanding of the 'panic' around children's gendered achievement,
- explore some of the reasons why these 'panics' have come about,
- consider the tensions that exist around the concept of 'school readiness' and whether there are gender implications in its use.

We will particularly focus on the panic that exists around boys' achievement within the UK education system. We will ask who is panicking and why. As we explore the concept of school readiness and gendered abilities to meet the Early Learning Goals, we will consider how boys' achievement in the Early Years contributes to their trajectory through the education system, making links with some key assessment points such as SATS, GCSEs and ultimately higher education entry. At the same time, we will return to the idea of intersectionality (Crenshaw, 2012) and consider whether the panic is about all boys or specific groups of boys. Furthermore, by using scripts that focus on boys' achievement, we will consider how discourses around girls' achievement can sometimes be silenced and also how these kinds of scripts position women teachers in a deficit way such as those who have feminised education to the detriment of boys (Ashley, 2003; Burn and Pratt-Adams, 2015; Skelton, 2012).

Are boys underachieving?

Before we consider whether the panic around boys' achievement is justified, we need to ascertain who is actually panicking and why there is a concern around boys' achievement. Is the 'panic' something whipped up by the media, as seen in the headlines above, or is there real evidence to cause people to be alarmed? We will consider documented evidence and data and then apply our own critique to what the data may be telling us. If we decide it is justifiable to worry about boys' experiences in the education system, then it is also important to consider when this concern should begin. For example, do we have to worry about this in the early years? Is there any evidence at the two-year progress check? At the Early Learning Goals? Or is it something that appears much later?

The alarmed

We note that a range of people and organisations are panicking about boys' achievement. Some of these include the government, parents, teachers and schools. Mostly the panic is driven by data which is drawn from statutory tests and assessments; these are used not just to look at children's gendered achievement and attainment but also to measure the performance of those who work with them.

Some charities in the UK context are concerned with how boys are progressing through the education system. For example, Save the Children (2016) published a report called 'The lost boys' which highlights the scale of the gender gap in literacy and language development; this exists even before children begin school. The report proceeds to examine the impact of this gap. The chosen title 'The lost boys' is particularly emotive, and the report justifies its use, continuing with impassioned word choice to assert: 'The difference in outcomes for boys and girls is having a *devastating* impact' (p. iv) and that this impact '*blights* childhoods' (p. v, our italics). The authors are talking about boys in the context of the UK as they offer their evidence but is there evidence from further afield to suggest that there are issues around boys' achievement across different countries and cultures?

It appears that others, further afield, are also panicking about boys' achievement; the OECD published a report in 2015 entitled 'The ABC of gender equality in education' (you may recall we suggested it as interesting further reading in Chapter 2 (Does a child's gender impact on how they play?)) to examine the differences in boys' and girls' achievement across 34 OECD countries and 30 partner countries (therefore 64 in total). They found some common threads such as 'high-performing' boys doing much better at maths and science than 'high-performing' girls, that achievement in science was generally equal and that girls read much more. Where they saw a clear panic was when they focused on children who might find learning more difficult, and in particular the:

> 15-year-old boys ... more likely than girls, on average, to fail to attain a baseline level of proficiency in reading, mathematics and science ... 14% of boys and 9% of girls surveyed by the PISA exercise did not attain the PISA baseline level of proficiency in any of the three core subjects.
>
> (OECD, 2015, p. 3)

Back to the UK context, this panic is also seen by other sources such as parents, schools and the government.

The internet is full of online debates among parents about whether it is harder to raise boys or girls; they offer anecdotal evidence on each side of the debate. Once the child starts school the debate is continued, as teachers look to address any gender imbalances in achievement. One of the reasons individual class teachers need to do this is because traditionally Ofsted have required information about this issue. However, recent updated guidance, which interestingly talks about a child's sex rather than their gender, has looked to change this focus, declaring:

> Performance differences between boys and girls ... are not included in inspection data summary reports (IDSR) ... While there can be differences between the performance of groups of pupils at a national level, this is likely to become meaningless when analysed at school level, particularly when there are small cohorts. Focusing on the underperformance of a particular group, in which data can be highly variable, can also have unintended consequences, such as unrealistic demands on schools and interventions based on analysis of very small groups of pupils.
>
> (Ofsted, 2019, p. 9)

However, at a national level the government certainly does look at these differences; every year the DfE publishes results of the SATS tests undertaken by children when they are aged 11. Unlike Ofsted, the DfE does use the terminology 'gender' and also highlights how girls 'continue to outperform boys' (Department for Education, 2018b). They state for example that '68% of girls reached the expected standard compared to 60% of boys'.

So, although the DfE's tone is more measured and factual than 'The lost boys' report, we can see from this data that it is not just the media that has concerns. It is noteworthy that the script used here is about reducing the gap between boys' and girls' achievement rather than reflecting critically on the suitability of the assessment for all children.

Therefore, although the word 'panic' may be considered too strong a word choice, we can suggest that there are varying degrees of concern, across a variety of sources and a variety of countries and cultures, regarding boys' engagement and achievement in formal education. This next section of the chapter will proceed to look in more detail at the actual concerns and the evidence that underpins them.

Issues to panic about

We have seen in the previous section that the scripts that surround the so-called panic often stem from a binary view comparing boys with girls; the end result is that girls are often seen to be coming out of the comparison better. Other scripts which then further arise from this end result position schools as feminised places, citing this situation as the reason that many boys fail to achieve effectively in such a gendered space. The argument goes that they are then further disadvantaged in life – can you see how difficult it is to move away from this stereotypically binary way to talk about boys and girls when it is seen everywhere in society?

Girls can appear to do better in the education system both in the UK and beyond. We only need to look at the evidence presented in the last section of this chapter to see how this assumption has come about. The concern around boys' achievement has become so great that some writers now refer to it as 'the boy problem' (Stoet, 2019) setting out how this is an issue at every stage of the education process in the UK including pre-primary, primary and secondary (ibid.). Lots of reasons are offered for this problem but perhaps the most controversial reason is the idea that education settings have become too feminised for boys to be able to effectively achieve in them.

So, let us look, then, at what people are writing about Early Years and this issue. Many writers (including Brownhill and Oates, 2016; Burn and Pratt-Adams, 2015; Cameron et al., 1999; Skelton, 2012) signpost the moral panic script around 'feminisation' and its impact on how boys both achieve in and engage with education. The term 'feminisation' has come to mean many things; in this context we borrow from Burn and Pratt-Adams (2015) to describe a way of teaching which has an 'assumed bias against boys' (p. 64). We could say that this type of pedagogy is especially prevalent in Early Years because the care element of this kind of work has been traditionally seen as the remit of women (Cameron et al., 1999). It is argued from this view point that female practitioners (and teachers) interact with children in specific ways, so it would benefit children to interact with male practitioners (and teachers) also. In this way, young children would benefit from a more diverse range of behaviours and practices (Rentzou, 2011). One criticism of the feminisation argument is that the raising of standards in education over the last 20 years has been done by a predominantly female workforce; they must be doing something right!

Another point that must be considered in this debate is what would be the opposite of over-feminised educational settings? If we are saying that this kind of setting is 'unfriendly' towards boys and their ways of learning, then we must in the same breath say what 'boy-friendly' settings would look like. A word of warning here: if you search online you will find many resources that discuss boy-friendly pedagogies. It's really important that you don't forget to critique these sources and try to find out their origins. For example, some are from religious organisations that have a particular traditional view of the role men and women should play in society and therefore have an interest in maintaining stereotypical scripts about men and women. Tim Oates was the chair of the National Curriculum committee which reviewed the recent overhaul of the national curriculum in the English context. One of the things he had to consider, of course, were the gender implications of the curriculum; he gave a keynote speech about these issues at Cambridge University (Oates, 2015) in which he emphasised:

- boys and girls benefit from the same strategies,
- tackling gender inequalities should begin at birth,
- more should be done early on to 'disrupt' gendered identities.

All in all, this was a clear call for the Early Years to focus on gender issues; hence the importance, we would argue, of this book.

TABLE 4.1 Taking responsibility for tackling gender inequalities

Action?	Whose responsibility?	Impact?

Time to consider

Oates (2015) suggests gender inequalities should be tackled from birth but what does that actually mean in practice and whose responsibility is it to do this? Try to complete a table like Table 4.1 to help you consider a response. Be as creative as you can!

Here is one final, but pertinent, thought to conclude this section of the chapter. We have considered carefully why different people and organisations are worrying about boys within the education system. It seems sad that at the same time we are not also celebrating girls and how, despite the many barriers to their success, they have really demonstrated that old-fashioned stereotypes of what girls are both allowed to do and are good at, have been dismantled for good.

Gendered early learning goals?

Recent educational debate has centred on how soon we should be assessing children's learning and development. For example, there is an intention in the English context to reintroduce baseline assessment in the first year of primary school (the reception class) to ensure both that children are school-ready, and that children's achievement can be closely tracked throughout their school career. The Early Learning Goals (ELGs) have been providing this information since 2001 so it would be interesting to see if they reveal any differences in gendered achievement.

Presently the ELGs are used in the English context to ascertain the readiness of a child to proceed to the formal learning of primary school. It is articulated that children will undertake these teacher assessments when they are five years old, at the end of the Early Years Foundation Stage; however, in reality, because reporting on children's achievement against these goals has to be finalised by the end of June, many children will still be four years old when they are assessed to see if they 'measure up'. Such a way of measuring and classifying children has not been without controversy. For example, Bradbury (2019) describes this approach as both 'datafication' and 'schoolification' of young children when she sets out the negative impact it can have. But is this a gendered impact and do the ELGs reveal differences between boys and girls at this young age?

To answer this question, we can look at the analysis of the data which is published every year by the DfE. At the time of writing (July 2019) it is too soon to look at this year's results; however, we can examine last year's (2018) and compare it to what happened previously. Girls are still consistently outperforming boys in terms of a good level of development although the gap between boys' and girls' achievement is reducing. For example, 2018 saw a gap of 13.5%, whereas in 2017 this was 13.7% and in 2014 it was 16.3%. The term 'good level of development' is closely tied to that of 'school readiness'; by having a 'good level of development' we are saying that a child is ready for school. Are we saying, then, that if you are born a girl you have more chance of being ready for school than if you are a boy? And if this is true, how does this then impact on a boy's journey through the education system?

Being 'school-ready' is an idea threaded throughout the Statutory Framework for the Early Years Foundation Stage (Department for Education, 2017). One definition the framework offers for this concept is 'the right foundation for good future progress through school and life' (p. 5). This foundation is provided by scoring a good level of development in the Early Learning Goals; those children who have not attained this level may have much more difficulty in making this transition. McBryde et al. (2004) draw on several sources to state that:

> Poor adjustment to starting school has been shown to have long-term and negative implications for future academic achievement (Reynolds, 1991; Entwistle and Alexander, 1998) and psychological well-being (Elizur, 1986) ... in this context there is a widely held view that "readying" children for school will enhance their transition (Kagan and Neuman, 1997).
>
> (p. 194)

Others have contested the concept of school readiness, such as the 'Too much too soon' campaign, which asserts that it should be schools that are ready for children rather than the other way around. This initiative was established by early childhood education experts to address the 'earlier and earlier start to formal instruction and an erosion of learning through play' (Whitebread and Jarvis, 2013, p. 1). Others have also contributed to this discussion about the transforming of childhood into a highly pressured preparation time for adulthood (House, 2011; Palmer, 2007) rather than a unique phase of a person's life in its own right.

Labelling, sorting and sifting children at the assessment of the Early Learning Goals may support school efficiency but it can be detrimental to children and can set them on a trajectory of disadvantage that they can then spend their whole life trying to escape. There are many reasons why a child may not achieve a good level of development and of course if performance at this stage of assessment highlights issues which can be picked up immediately, before they have had chance to develop into something that can impact negatively on a child's life, then this is all well and good. However, other countries do not find it necessary to label children at such a young age. It is particularly problematic if other issues, such as gender, may prevent children from really demonstrating what they know and what they can do, instead forcing them to be positioned in a deficit way early in their lives.

To summarise this section of the chapter, we remind you that there is global data to suggest that boys are underachieving and it is on the educational agenda of many countries worldwide to tackle this underachievement. Parents, school leaders, charities and policymakers are among those who are leading on this concern. Their so-called 'panic' is around boys' disaffection with education and the knock-on effect this has on their achievement. In the English context this underachievement is already seen at five years old when children are assessed against the Early Learning Goals. On the international stage this is seen at 15 years old when many countries take part in the PISA tests.

Time to consider

Think back to your own early school days. Do you remember any ideas you had about things that girls were good at or things that boys were noticed for? For example, we can remember 'naughty' boys who were always getting into trouble but we can't remember any 'naughty' girls. We remember the names of boys who were 'good at' computers and maths but we don't remember girls being specifically praised by the teacher for this. What about you? What do you recall? It's important to examine how some of our early understanding about learning success was formed and then consider whether it impacts at all on the way that we might look at children today.

Do children have gendered journeys through the education system?

An early achievement gap is identified in the English education system; other differences appear when we reflect on educational choices children make when they are allowed to select school subjects. These choices subsequently inform what young adults choose to study for a higher education degree. However, we cannot claim that children have gendered journeys through the education system without returning to the notion of intersectionality (Crenshaw, 2012) and asking whether the so-called panic is about all boys or just a 'certain kind of boys'. Furthermore, we also need to turn the spotlight on girls and examine more closely what is happening to them in the education system.

SATS, GCSES, A levels and higher education

In this last section of this chapter we consider achievement at the early stages of formal education. In this part, let's see what happens at the ages of 7 (Key Stage 1 SATS), 11 (Key Stage 2 SATS), 16 (GCSEs), 18 (A levels) and 21+ (University degree).

In England, children undertake SATs tests when they are in Year 2 (six–seven years old). These tests are then marked by the class teacher and used in at least three ways: (1) to inform parents about their child's progress, (2) to set performance management targets for class teachers and (3) to track children's progress through school. These results are then reported, and compared, nationally. At the time of writing (July 2019) the 2019 results have not been analysed but we can look at the 2018 results and notice these gender differences:

> More girls reached the expected standard than boys in all KS1 TA [Teacher Assessed] subjects. The subject with the largest difference in attainment by gender continued to be writing, with a gap of 13 percentage points between girls (77%) and boys (63%). The gender attainment gap was nine percentage points in reading, with 80% of girls and 71% of boys reaching the standard. The gap was narrowest for maths at two percentage points, where 77% of girls reached the standard compared to 75% of boys ....
> (Department for Education, 2018a)

SATs tests are also taken for those in their last year of primary school; they are not marked by the teacher but sent away to be marked externally. Schools then receive the results by the beginning of July and the results are analysed by the DfE, and made public, later on in the year. We already noted earlier in this chapter that the analysis of the 2018 results highlight similar gaps to those seen at Key Stage 1.

In the English context, when pupils are 11 years old, they transition into the secondary school system; their attainment does not then become public property until the success they have achieved at GCSE level (usually when they are 16) is reported and compared. Generally, two years before taking these exams they are given some choice around subjects they would like to study further and some they no longer wish to pursue. If we look at these choices through a gender lens, we can definitely see some differences. For example, Knott (2018) offers a useful analysis of choices in 2018 and reveals:

> Music is one of several arts subjects from which boys are turning away at a faster rate than girls ... by 2017/18, female entries outnumbered male entries by almost 4,000. The tendency for boys to dominate GCSE entries for design and technology (DT) has also dramatically intensified ... By 2017/18, the gender gap had increased by 16 percentage points, with 67% of entries from boys

and 33% from girls ... In 2013/14, 38% of drama entries were from males and 62% were from females. By 2017/18, the figures were 37% of entrants and 63% respectively ... gender ratios in art and design GCSE have largely held firm. Girls continue to dominate entries ... accounting for ... 67% [of exam sittings] in 2017/18 ... The proportions of boys and girls taking physics, chemistry, biology and maths has remained steady, at about 50% for both genders ... the proportion of female entries [for computing] has risen from 15% to 20%.

Knott offers the useful information just quoted in terms of gendered subject choice, but once pupils have made these choices what does their gendered achievement look like? Since new exams were introduced in 2018 for GCSEs, there seems to have been a positive impact for boys – more of them (17.1%) have achieved the very top marks. However, this is still less than the percentage of girls who achieve the highest marks which in 2018 was 23.4% (Adams and Barr, 2018).

These gender decisions in subject choices and then subsequent attainment can often be offered as a rationale for single-sex schools (there's that problematic word 'sex' again!). We know, for example that gender impacts on choice of subject when pupils go on to make A-level choices. Just look at the subjects of psychology and English in 2016; we know that 76% of those who studied the former were girls as were 73% of the latter (Kirke, 2016). We also know that in the same year an astonishing nine out of ten who took computing at A level were male. If we look at choices made by those who attend single-sex schools, we see some interesting things happen, with girls more likely to both take, and achieve well in, traditional male subjects such as physics (Sullivan, 2009) and boys more likely to feel confident about their ability to achieve in English (Menzies, 2016).

If we look for gender differences, we will find them at each stage of a child's educational journey from infant to young adult. The differences are apparent both in subject choice and in attainment.

Time to consider

What do you think about single-sex schooling or classes? This is an argument that emerges again and again. Consider first the term 'single-sex school'; what assumptions is such a term making about sex and gender? Think about your own experiences; perhaps you were educated in a 'single-sex' way. If so, consider how this may have formed your beliefs about your own capacity to learn. What if you went instead to a mixed school? How might this have helped you form certain beliefs? Make two lists – one for the benefits of single-sex schooling, one for the drawbacks. Who benefits? Who is disadvantaged? And where do you stand on this issue?

Case study

When Jerome begins school, two days after his fourth birthday, his teacher carries out a baseline assessment. She uses the results of this to place him in a lower-ability group. Jerome continues in his ability set throughout his educational career until he leaves school at 16 with only a handful of GCSEs. However, after successfully completing some Level 3 qualifications at college, he gains excellent A levels and is able to enrol at the university of his choice. He reflects back on his learning journey and reflects on what went wrong and what went right for him.

Possible response

Do you remember the game of snakes and ladders? Try to imagine Jerome's journey as plotted on such a game board and note down some of the snakes (e.g. summer-born) and some of the ladders (rejection of low-ability labels) as he progresses through the education system.

Final reflection

There is a panic, not just in the UK context but worldwide, around boys' achievement. However, it is certainly not all boys we are panicking about – just certain groups of them within society, so we must look at ideas around intersectionality (Crenshaw, 2012) rather than just gender. We are right to panic if we are setting up any child to fail within the education system.

Key points

- There has been a consistent concern about boys' achievement within the education system both in the UK context and beyond.
- In the English context this begins very early when children are five and are assessed against the Early Learning Goals.
- School readiness is a key goal in the English education system; the ELGs reveal that boys are less ready than girls.

Further reading

1. Save the Children (2016) *The lost boys*. Available at: https://resourcecentre.savethechildren.net/node/10,031/pdf/the_lost_boys_report.pdf (accessed: 11th July 2019).

    Read the above report and consider how they assert that boys are disadvantaged even before they begin school.

2 Skelton, C. (2012) 'Men teachers and the "feminised" primary school: A review of the literature', *Educational Review*, 64(1), pp. 1–19.

Consider how the ideas that Skelton unearths in the research literature regarding primary schools could also apply to early years.

References

Adams, R. and Barr, C. (2018) *GCSEs: Boys close gap on girls after exams overhaul*. Available at: www.theguardian.com/education/2018/aug/23/gcses-boys-close-gap-on-girls-after-exams-overhaul. (accessed: 21st August 2019).

Ashley, M. (2003) 'Primary schoolboys' identity formation and the male role model: An exploration of sexual identity and gender identity in the UK through attachment theory', *Sex Education*, 3(3), pp. 257–270.

Bradbury, A. (2019) 'Datafied at four: The role of data in the 'schoolification' of early childhood education in England', *Learning, Media and Technology*, 44(1), pp. 7–21.

Brownhill, S. and Oates, R. (2016) 'Who do you want me to be? An exploration of female and male perceptions of 'imposed' gender roles in the early years'. *Education 3–13*. 45(5), pp. 658–670.

Burn, E. and Pratt-Adams, S. (2015) *Men Teaching Children 3–11: Dismantling Gender Barriers*. London: Bloomsbury.

Cameron, C., Moss, P. and Owen, C. (1999) *Men in the Nursery*. London: Paul Chapman.

Cohen, S. (2002) *Folk Devils and Moral Panics: Volume 9 (Routledge Classics)*. Taylor and Francis. Kindle Edition.

Crenshaw, K. (2012) *On Intersectionality: Essential Writings*. Jackson, TN: Perseus.

Department for Education (2017) *Statutory framework for the early years foundation stage*. Available at: www.foundationyears.org.uk/files/2017/03/EYFS_STATUTORY_FRAMEWORK_2017.pdf (accessed: 21st August 2019).

Department for Education (2018a) *National curriculum assessments at key stage 1 and phonics screening checks in England, 2018*. Available at: www.gov.uk/government/publications/phonics-screening-check-and-key-stage-1-assessments-england-2018/national-curriculum-assessments-at-key-stage-1-and-phonics-screening-checks-in-england-2018 (accessed: 21st August 2019).

Department for Education (2018b) *National curriculum assessments at key stage 2 in England, 2018*. Available from: www.gov.uk/government/publications/national-curriculum-assessments-key-stage-2-2018-provisional/national-curriculum-assessments-at-key-stage-2-in-england-2018-provisional–2#gender-gaps (accessed: 21st August 2019).

House, R. (2011) *Too Much, Too Soon? Early Learning and the Erosion of Childhood (Early Years)*. Gloucestershire: Hawthorn Press.

Kirke, A. (2016) *A-level results 2016: Which subjects did students do the best and worst in?* Available from: www.telegraph.co.uk/education/2016/08/18/a-level-results-2016-which-subjects-did-students-do-the-best-and/ (accessed: 21st August 2019).

Knott, J. (2018) *EBacc blamed for growing gender imbalance in GCSE choices*. Available at: www.artsprofessional.co.uk/news/ebacc-blamed-growing-gender-imbalance-gcse-choices (accessed: 21st August 2019).

McBryde, C., Ziviani, J. and Cuskelly, M. (2004) 'School readiness and factors that influence decision making', *Occupational Therapy International*, 11(4), pp. 193–208.

Menzies, L. (2016) *Ethnicity, gender and social mobility: New report*. Available from: www.lkmco.org/ethnicity-gender-social-mobility-new-report (accessed: 21st August 2019).

Oates, T. (2015) *Boy-friendly teaching 'will not tackle gender divide'*. Available at: www.cambridgeassessment.org.uk/news/boy-friendly-teaching-will-not-tackle-gender-divide-tim-oates-cbe (accessed: 21st August 2019).

OECD (2015) *The ABC of gender equality in education*. Available at: www.oecd.org/pisa/keyfindings/pisa-2012-results-gender-eng.pdf (accessed: 21st August 2019).

Ofsted (2019) School inspection update. Available at: https://assets.publishing.service.gov.uk/government/uploads/system/uploads/attachment_data/file/814954/School_inspection_update_July_2019.pdf (accessed: 21st August 2019).

Palmer, S. (2007) *Toxic Childhood*. London: Orion.

Pells, R. (2016) 'Tory MP claims boys are disadvantaged by "over-feminised" school system'. *The Independent*. [online] 10 September. Accessed 25th November 2019. Available from: https://www.independent.co.uk/news/education/education-news/karl-mccartney-tory-mp-claims-boys-disadvantaged-over-feminised-gender-gap-school-system-a7235761.htm

Rentzou, K. (2011) 'Greek parents' perceptions of male early childhood educators', *Early Years: An International Research Journal*, 31(2), pp. 135–147.

Save the Children (2016) The Lost Boys. Available at: https://resourcecentre.savethechildren.net/node/10031/pdf/the_lost_boys_report.pdf (accessed: 21st July 2019).

Skelton, C. (2012) 'Men teachers and the "feminised" primary school: A review of the literature', *Educational Review*, 64(1), pp. 1–19.

Smith, A. (2006) 'Feminised curriculum "has thrown boys out with bathwater"'. *The Guardian*. [online] 13 June. Accessed 25th November 2019. Available from: https://www.theguardian.com/education/2006/jun/13/schools.uk3

Stoet, G. (2019) 'The challenges for boys and men in twenty-first-century education'. in: J.A. Barry, R. Kingerlee, M. Seager and L. Sullivan (eds) *The Palgrave Handbook of Male Psychology and Mental Health*. London: Palgrave.

Sullivan, A. (2009) 'Academic self-concept, gender and single-sex schooling', *British Educational Research Journal*, 35(2), pp. 259–288.

Vine, S. (2016) 'The betrayal of our boys'. *The Daily Mail*. [online] 26 May. Accessed 25th November 2019. Available from: https://www.dailymail.co.uk/debate/article-3609832/The-betrayal-boys-falling-girls-way-says-SARAH-VINE-feminisation-society-especially-schools-blame.html

Whitebread, D. and Jarvis, P. (2013) *Too Much Too Soon: Reflections upon the school starting age*. Available at: www.toomuchtoosoon.org (accessed: 21st August 2019).

PART

II

A gendered workforce

CHAPTER 5

Why is there a gender imbalance in the early years workforce?

Introduction

We are now starting a new section of the book. Part I focussed on the gendered child; we considered how individual children may be constrained by the gendered practices of those around them and society as a whole. Many birth to five-year-olds, in the English context, now attend formal ECEC settings; therefore, it is relevant to turn our gaze towards these settings, and, in particular, the adults who are working there. We have already touched on the fact that these adults are predominantly female; in this section of the book we will explore this issue much further by considering how this situation has come about and also the impact it could have. To begin the discussion this chapter will:

- build your understanding of why there is currently an unequal gender balance in the early years workforce,
- explore some of the historical, political reasons as to why this has come about,
- highlight how this gender imbalance mirrors stereotypical perceptions of men and women in wider society.

As this chapter examines the unequal gender balance in the early years workforce (Mistry and Sood, 2015; Rentzou, 2011), considering how it has come about, it will unpick some of the 'common-sense cultural binaries' (Robinson and Jones Diaz, 2016, p. 32) we use that contribute to this situation. We will reflect on some of the new and emerging evidence around this issue as policymakers' growing interest and concern becomes apparent. The chapter will also consider why some discourses about Early Years are seen as more truthful than others and how this relates both to questions of power (Foucault, 1998) and the reinforcing of stereotypes, particularly around the issue of 'women's work' (Lupton, 2000).

Gender balance or imbalance?

Have you ever worked, volunteered or visited an early years setting in the UK? Have a quick think – how many female practitioners did you see? And how many male ones? Those of you who have experience in early years settings won't be surprised to hear that there is a gender imbalance in the early years workforce in the UK and beyond. For example, men make up only 2% of the early years workforce in England. This figure remained static between 2008 and 2013 (Department for Education, 2017) and the Fatherhood Institute (2017) argue that it has not increased since. Now think about the children who go to early years settings – is there a gender imbalance of ECEC attendees? No, of course there's not. But there is a large proportion of children in England attending early years settings: in England, 94% of three- and four-year-olds received funding to attend an ECEC setting in 2018, alongside 72% of two-year-olds (Department for Education, 2018). However, with men making up only 2% of practitioners, that means the majority of those children will only have experiences with female early years practitioners. Take a moment to think about this. Do you think that that's a concern? Should we be worried about this?

Some people are worrying about this, and a moral panic has developed about the low percentage of men in ECEC. The government has expressed a desire to tackle this; they believe that increasing the number of male ECEC practitioners will help to address the lower levels of academic achievement of boys in comparison to girls, to minimise the impact of absent fathers, to develop pedagogic practices in schools and settings, and to promote 'male' behaviours in children (Brownhill and Oates, 2016, p. 3). Here we want to reiterate the problematic nature of gender – is it the case that more men are seen as necessary in early years settings because they can provide something above and beyond that of female practitioners? We need to be wary of falling into that trap of thinking because we don't want to adopt a deficit model of the women who make up the vast majority of the early years workforce.

You might think that the government's desire for more men in ECEC is relatively recent, as the percentage of male practitioners has remained so low and so static since 2008. Yet this isn't the case. Back in 1998 The National Childcare Strategy set a target to increase the recruitment of men to ECEC settings to 6% by 2004, though this was abandoned when the target wasn't reached (Roberts-Holmes, 2013). Then in 2010 the coalition government made a commitment to 'a greater gender balance in the early years workforce' (p. 19) as part of an aim to support free early years education. Most recently, in 2017 the Department for Education (2017) published their Early Years Workforce Strategy, which also wants to promote a more gender-balanced workforce, arguing that 'we want children in early years provision to have both male and female role models to guide them in their early years, and we want more men to choose to work in the early years sector' (2017, p. 24). Again, as Brownhill and Oates (2016) suggest, their rationale for this current aim is underpinned by research carried out by the Children's Development and Workforce Council in 2008 that '17% of children from lone parent families had fewer than two hours a week of contact time with a man, whilst 36% had under six hours' (Department for Education, 2017, p24). The government uses this as evidence that male ECEC practitioners are necessary to ensure that children are able to have access to quality time with men. And, much further back in time, the Plowden report (1967), which was seen as the 'first major report into primary education since the Hadow reports of the 1930s' (Kingdon, 2014, p. 77), comments on the small amount of male primary school teachers and makes recommendations for increasing the number. The report states that 'in infant schools in 1965 there were only 97 brave men out of a total of 33,000 teachers' (CACE, 1967, p. 313) with later claims that:

> there are both educational and practical grounds for urging that as far as possible there should be men teachers in all primary schools. Some young children, particularly boys, may respond better to teaching from a man than from a woman, and most schools and communities benefit from the contributions of both men and women teachers. It is also clear that a staff on which there are men teachers is likely to be more stable than a staff made up exclusively of women
> (Central Advisory Council for Education (CACE), 1967, p. 324).

The lack of male ECEC practitioners isn't just an issue in the UK; female-dominated early years workforces exist across the world. Peeters et al. (2015) suggest that in Europe there are only three countries – Norway, Denmark and Turkey – where at least 5% of the ECEC workforce are male. But what is promising is that evidence from other European countries illustrates that it is possible to increase the number of men working in ECEC – in Norway the amount of male ECEC practitioners tripled between 2000 and 2013 and thus the percentage of male workers increased from 5% to almost 9% in the same time period (Peeters et al., 2015). However, what is frustrating is that although we know what actions were taken to increase the number of male ECEC practitioners, including allocating money for supporting recruitment, creating networks for male practitioners and the commitment to recruit male practitioners in Government Action Plans for Gender Equality, Peeters et al. (2015) suggest that there isn't clear evidence on which measures have been effective in helping Norway increase their percentage of male practitioners.

Time to consider

What measures do you think might be most effective in increasing the number of male practitioners? Can you find any research that has been written since Peeters et al. (2015) published their article that might explain how men can be attracted to work in ECEC?

How has the gender imbalance come about?

In Chapter 4 (Does a child's gender impact on how they achieve?) we considered the panic about boys particularly in the education system and said one of the panics is about the fact that the education system has become feminised. You might think that this has always been the case but it is believed that before the introduction of mass state schooling in 1870 there were about even numbers of male and female teachers (Partington, 1976 cited in Skelton, 2012). Burn and Pratt-Adams (2015) talk about how the first infant teachers were 'radical young men' out to change society. In fact, the first infant school in Britain was set up by a man – Robert Owen. And rather than choosing teachers based on their gender they were selected by their qualities; his key considerations were 'good temper, patience and a strong love of children' (Bradburn, 1966, p. 59). Similarly, 'arguably the most significant of the pioneers of early childhood education and care' was also male – Friedrich Froebel (Tovey, 2017, p. 1). So rather than the workforce always being female-dominated, this has changed over the course of the last 150 years.

Over time the workforce has changed to become predominantly made up of women. What is more is that Froebel may have contributed to this in two ways. Firstly, Froebel himself believed that women were 'ideally equipped for [working in the kindergarten] because they possessed an innate maternal tendency' (Hirsh and Hilton, 2000, p. 12). Take a moment to consider this – is this something that you believe, too? Do you think other people like practitioners and parents might agree with Froebel that women have something innate that makes them suitable for working with young children – something that men do not possess? Secondly, Hirsh and Hilton (2000) talk about how Froebelian ideologies fitted with wider 'social motherhood' endeavours that liberal middle-class women were engaging in, which was 'already an important rhetorical strategy sanctioning women's authority in the public domain' (p. 13). Essentially what that means is that some middle-class women had got hold of the ideas of Frobel and other pioneers and realised that leading the way in sharing these philosophies was a role they could do to give them prominence. An informal network of middle-class women across Europe and the US was set up, which facilitated women to access training, experience and employment (Read, 2003). Through this, some women were able to carve a niche position for themselves and make Froebelian principles their forte. One of these women was Margaret McMillan, recognised as one of the pioneers of early childhood education in the UK. She was influenced by Froebel's thinking and served on the Council of the National Froebel Society. In line with Froebel's beliefs that women had a significant role to play in the kindergarten, in 1919 McMillan established a training school for young girls to become the natural 'nurturers of small children' (Steedman, 1990, p. 83, cited in Burn and Pratt-Adams, 2015).

There are wider historical and political reasons why women have come to be in the majority in teaching young children. Burn and Pratt-Adams (2015) consider some of these, for instance citing Tropp (1957, p. 208) that shortly after the turn of the 19th century the way that teachers were trained and recruited changed, which hindered how quickly they earnt and had impact on how many people decided to join the workforce, leading to a fall in male recruits in particular. Following this, the start of World War One in 1914 led to male teachers becoming almost extinct, and although the number of male teachers picked up following the end of the war (in part because of the introduction of 'marriage bars', which banned women from working as teachers once they got married), following the start of World War Two the number of female teachers increased once again.

So, with government efforts to foster more men to work in early childhood, why does an unequal gender balance persist? You might think that it's because the people predominantly paying for early years education – parents – don't want men to work with young children. Yet research from the Pre-school Learning Alliance (2011) found that in fact 98% of parents were in favour of men working in childcare with three- to five-year-olds, and over 90% of parents approved of men working with babies, toddlers and two-year-olds. When surveyed in 2003, only 77% of British parents were in favour of men working in ECEC, which shows how attitudes to male practitioners are changing (IPSOS MORI, 2003).

Rentzou (2011) cites IPSOS MORI in her research exploring what parents think about men working in early childhood in Greece. She states that, on the whole, the parents who participated in her study were also in favour of male early childhood educators and also in favour of increasing the number of men working with young children. However, the parents did identify barriers to this happening. For instance, they indicated that, in the Greek context, society may feel uneasy about men's motives for working with young children and those recruiting may think it 'risky to hire males' (2011, p. 143). Rentzou's study also found that parents believe that men may be put off working in ECEC because of the low salary and career potential, the possibility of feeling isolated, concerns that they will not be trusted and also concerns that allegations of child abuse may be made against them.

These beliefs from parents echo some of the findings from Mistry and Sood (2015) who conducted research with a small sample of 18 male trainee primary school teachers and 13 male primary school head teachers. They wanted to find out: (a) what male trainee teachers thought about gender stereotyping within their role, (b) what the challenges were with addressing these stereotypes and (c) what school leaders could do to address such stereotypes. Just like the parents in Rentzou's (2011) research suspected, male trainee teachers feared being wrongly accused of inappropriate behaviour against children and also expressed views of feeling isolated and 'like the outsider' (2015, p. 120). We will come back to this research later on in the chapter.

What influences society's perceptions of men working in ECEC?

So far in this chapter we have considered how the gender imbalance in the ECEC workforce has changed over time and some of the reasons why men currently do not choose careers which involve caring for young children. We have suggested that a major problem is linked to stereotypes around the male practitioner. It is important, at this point, to consider where these stereotypes come from and what their basis is from a theoretical point of view. Therefore, in this section we are going to think about the work of Connell (2016), Robinson and Jones Diaz (2016) and also the theories of Foucault to help us understand how policies and practices around men working in ECEC are shaped.

Firstly, let's have a look at Connell (2016). Do you remember we introduced her as a seminal theorist in Chapter 1? Her work is useful to consider because it helps us understand how the gender issues in the ECEC workforce relate to other gender issues. She talks about the different levels on which we can think about gender. For instance, often people talk about gender on a small scale, in relation to things like their relationships and families. We can refer to these types of dealings with gender as being on the 'micro' level. For instance, on a micro level you might want to think about the role that gender has played in your life this week – has anyone made a remark to you, complimentary or not, based on your gender? But Connell argues that it is important to consider gender on a global scale as well (i.e. the 'macro' level), for instance in relation to things like femicide or female genital mutilation (FGM). She suggests that it is the same issues of 'gendered power', or patriarchy, which impact on both these micro and macro events. It is helpful to think about Connell's ideas as a continuum (Figure 5.1); we can place the micro everyday matters at one end of the continuum and the macro world-scale matters at the other. The world of ECEC then fits somewhere on this continuum between these two extremes.

Thinking about gender issues in this way shows how they are all connected and that the gender issues within the ECEC workforce will be influenced by both the small everyday issues and the larger global issues. Similarly, issues along the continuum will be influenced by ECEC. We know that the values and beliefs that young children are instilled with in early childhood settings will have an impact on how they go on to shape the world as young people and adults.

Global Issues   Everyday Issues

FIGURE 5.1 'Thinking-about-gender' continuum (adapted from Connell, 2016)

One way of considering how the gender issues on the continuum interconnect in relation to the ECEC workforce is by thinking about the role that discourses and scripts play. We introduced this idea in Chapter 1 and are going to explore it further here. If you look up these two words in a dictionary, you'll find that they both relate to communication, discussion and debate. We like to think about discourses as being related to *the stories that are told about something* and scripts as being related to *the ways of talking* that are used. Robinson and Jones Diaz (2016) say that the discourses (scripts) we use to talk about gender will impact on 'polices and practices' at a more macro level.

That means that the stories we tell about gender in everyday contexts will influence what is said about gender issues on a bigger scale. Think back to what we said about the ideas of Froebel earlier on in this chapter, as this might help you understand this a little better. The discourse Froebel communicated was that women possess something innate about caring and educating that men do not. The impact of this discourse was that policies and practices developed to recognise the need for women in the ECEC workforce – for instance how Margaret McMillan set up a training centre for young women to become early childhood educators based on this belief. Robinson and Jones Diaz call the way we talk about gender as 'normalizing discourses' (2016, p. 45). If we come back to our idea of discourses as being like stories that are told, then 'normalising discourses' are like a rumour being repeated and therefore gaining traction, power and belief.

So how are discourses having an impact on the gender imbalance in the ECEC workforce? Thinking back to the previous section, we considered how people like Rentzou (2011) and Mistry and Sood (2015) talk about how one potential barrier for recruiting male practitioners is the stereotypes that are shared about men in the ECEC workforce. For instance, one male trainee teacher participant expressed that there are stereotypes from society that 'males should not be in EY, and if they are then they have an ulterior motive' (2015, p. 122). The discourses and scripts that are used around these stereotypes can strengthen these barriers and make the stereotypes harder to challenge. The Fatherhood Institute also talk about the barriers of stereotypes placed on male practitioners, for instance that they should do the stereotypical male activities like football and be responsible for parental engagement with fathers and other male family members (Fatherhood Institute, 2015).

The ideas of the French philosopher Michel Foucault are helpful to consider when thinking about discourses. He was interested in issues of power and the idea that power isn't held by one person, but instead 'power is everywhere' (Foucault, 1998, p. 63). He coined the concept of 'regimes of truth'. Let's take a moment to think about what this term might mean. 'Regime' is another word for 'rule' or 'establishment'. In brief, a society's regimes of truth are the discourses that it accepts. The people with power will be the people who influence those regimes of truth. So, if we think back to what Connell (2016) believes about gender issues and patriarchy, we could say that the regimes of truth and the accepted discourses are shaped by patriarchy. Foucault himself defines discourses as 'practices that systematically form the objects of which they speak' (1974, p. 49). In other words, by talking about things we make them real; for example, by talking about gender differences we make them real.

Foucault was also interested in identity, otherness and inequalities. We can link all of these concepts to the gender imbalance of the ECEC workforce to help us understand how the discourse around men working in ECEC has been developed:

- issues of power: i.e. patriarchy,
- issues of identity: i.e. gender,
- issues of otherness: i.e. male and female,
- issues of inequalities: i.e. the ECEC workforce.

Related to this, Robinson and Jones Diaz look at the theory of discourse in the context of Early Years. They say we all have our own discourses to talk about and explain ideas and issues in our everyday life. As we talk about them they are perpetuated, i.e. they become reinforced and consolidated. They also say that in these discourses we often use 'common-sense binaries' which we don't critically challenge. They give some examples as being:

- Male – Female,
- Black – White,
- Heterosexual – Homosexual,
- Western – Non-western,
- Adult – Child.

Robinson and Jones Diaz also challenge us to think about why some discourses are seen as more truthful than others. Once again, we have to come back to this idea of power; they say that if a discourse is taken up by a powerful institution then it becomes true. They give the example of child immunisation. The problem is that discourses are not neutral; not only are they given power, but they reproduce power that reinforces privilege. So, we could say that just as the immunisation discourse privileges the big drug companies. In a similar way, gender discourses privileges patriarchy.

Time to consider

Examine the 'common-sense binaries' from Robinson and Jones Diaz (2016, p. 33). Are some 'truer' than others? Have some of them changed in terms of how true they are? What do they tell us about who is holding the power in that discourse?

What are the implications of gendered discourses for the workforce and for young children?

There are several implications for the gender discourses that exist in relation to men in the ECEC workforce in the UK. One is that looking after young children continues to be seen as women's work (Lupton, 2000). Such discourses may also contribute to perceptions of ECEC work as low status and therefore only worthy of low pay. It might be argued that the lack of men working in ECEC, which is as a result of the gender discourse that exists, means that there are pedagogies that are missing or sidelined in early childhood settings, although our next chapter (Chapter 6: What is the impact of the gender imbalance in the early years workforce?) offers some evidence against this. And it may lead to a passing on of the cultural baton of how to be a man and how to be a woman (Rogoff, 1990) so that gender stereotypes continue to be reinforced.

But in other parts of the world there are discourses which exist that aim to encourage a more gender-balanced workforce. Peeters et al. (2015) suggest that in Norway there's a discourse that men are important in ECEC, which centres around three arguments. Firstly, there is the argument that men are important in children's lives. Secondly, there is the argument that Norwegian laws and curricula strive for gender equality. Thirdly, there is the argument that a gender-balanced workforce is necessary in ECEC in order to give young children a stimulating and pedagogical environment (2015, p. 304). This shows that discourses and scripts can be challenged and can evolve over time.

Case study

Geoff is 14 and is planning his Year 10 work experience. He has lots of younger cousins and really enjoys looking after them and entertaining them at family parties. Everyone tells him how great he is with young children although it hasn't crossed his mind that working with them could be a possible career choice; he is adamant he does not want to be a primary school teacher, for example. He is disappointed to only be offered a small number of work experience opportunities to choose from, such as shadowing in a garden centre or the local car mechanic. When he chats to his friends over lunch, he discovers that two of them, Lucy and Sally, are going to the local day nursery. He thinks he would have liked to have been given this opportunity if only to find out what working with young children is like. Have a think about Geoff's case study; does his experience resonate with your own, or any of your friends or family? We have found through talking to our very few male Early Childhood Studies students that this has been normal practice for them. How does their (and Geoff's) experience link with the idea of discourses and of power? Is there anything that Geoff can do to disrupt this kind of discourse and subsequent practices?

Possible response

If Geoff does not share his views beyond his conversation with his friends, then there is a danger that it will take a very long time to disrupt the script about suitable gendered work experience presently existing in his school. Geoff needs to be encouraged and supported to share his views with a school professional who understands the gendered implications and who can support him to ensure that in future his school ceases to make assumptions about work experience based on outmoded ideas about gender. Geoff, and young men like him, needs to be given the opportunity to consider that working with young children is a viable career choice before they rule it out.

Final reflection

In this chapter we have considered the gendered nature of the early years workforce and the fact that children mostly engage with women in the early years setting. We have thought about gender discourses which are used to explain why more men should, or should not, be in the early years workforce and begun to consider the implications of having such a highly gendered workforce. In the next chapter we will explore much further what the impact of the gender imbalance might be and then in Chapter 7 (How can we achieve a more gender-balanced workforce?) what can be done about this situation.

Key points

- There is a significant gender imbalance in the ECEC workforce; in England about 98% of the workforce is female. The most gender-balanced country in Europe is Norway, in which around 9% of the ECEC workforce is male.
- It's important to reflect upon why there is such a stark gender imbalance in the UK ECEC workforce. One reason is that the discourses that we use to talk about gender create stereotypes that can act as a barrier to men working in early childhood. Some discourses are seen to hold more weight than others, because of the issue of power.
- The discourses around gender impact the ECEC workforce and children in other ways too. These discourses may have implications for how the workforce is seen and how the roles of men and women are seen. But they aren't universal; different countries have different gender discourses.

Further reading

1 Mistry, M. and Sood, K. (2015) 'Why are there still so few men within early years in primary schools: Views from male trainee teachers and male leaders?', *Education 3–13*, 43(2), pp. 115–127.

It's worth having a look at Mistry and Sood's (2015) piece of research exploring the views of male primary school trainee teachers and head teachers about gender stereotyping within their profession.

2 Peeters, J., Rohrmann, T. and Emilsen, K. (2015) 'Gender balance in ECEC: Why is there so little progress?', *European Early Childhood Education Research Journal*, 23(3), pp. 302–314. doi: 10.1080/1350293X.2015.1043805.

Peeters et al.'s (2015) have written a really interesting article that looks at what is happening in Belgium, Turkey, Norway and Germany with regards to recruitment of male practitioners and explores why progress might be slow in addressing the gender imbalance.

References

Bradburn, E. (1966) 'Britain's first nursery-infant school', *The Elementary School Journal*, 67(2), pp. 57–63.

Brownhill, S. and Oates, R. (2016) 'Who do you want me to be? an exploration of female and male perceptions of 'imposed' gender roles in the early years', *Education 3–13*, doi: 10.1080/03004279.2016.1164215.

Burn, E. and Pratt-Adams, S. (2015) *Men Teaching Children 3:11: Dismantling Gender Barriers*. London: Bloomsbury.

Central Advisory Council for Education (CACE) (1967) *Children and Their Primary Schools ('The Plowden Report')*. London: HMSO.

Connell, R.W. (2016) '100 million Kalashnikovs: Gendered power on a world scale', *Debate Feminista*, 51, pp. 3–17.

Department for Education (2017) *Early years workforce strategy*. Available at: https://gov.uk/government/uploads/system/uploads/attachment_data/file/596884/Workforce_strategy_02-03-2017.pdf (accessed: 8th February 2019).

Department for Education (2018) *Provision for Children Under Five Years of Age in England, January 2018*. Available at: https://assets.publishing.service.gov.uk/government/uploads/system/uploads/attachment_data/file/719273/Provision_for_children_under_5_2018_-_text.pdf (accessed: 8th February 2019).

Fatherhood Institute (2015) *Men in Childcare: How Can We Achieve a More Gender-Balanced Early Years and Childcare Workforce?* Available at: http://fatherhoodinstitute.org/wp-content/uploads/2015/04/Men-into-Childcare-PDF.pdf (accessed: 23rd February 2019).

Fatherhood Institute (2017) *How can we attract more men into London's early years workforce?* Available at: http://fatherhoodinstitute.org/wp-content/uploads/2017/09/MITEY-2017-London-report-1.pdf (accessed: 8th February 2019).

Foucault, M. (1974) *The Archaeology of Knowledge*. London: Tavistock. TNT.
Foucault, M. (1998) *The History of Sexuality: The Will to Knowledge*. London: Penguin.
Hirsh, P. and Hilton, M. (2002) *Practical Visionaries: Women, Education and Social Progress, 1790-1930*. London: Routledge.
IPSOS MORI (2003) *Men and Childcare*. Available at: https://ipsos.com/ipsos-mori/en-uk/men-and-childcare (accessed: 15th February 2019).
Kingdon, Z. (2014) 'The early years foundation stage: Tickell and beyond: A critical perspective', in: Z. Kingdon and J. Gourd (eds) *Early Years Policy: The impact on Practice*. Oxon: Routledge. pp. 75–94.
Lupton, B. (2000) 'Maintaining masculinity: Men who do 'women's work'', *British Journal of Management*, 11, pp. 33–48.
Mistry, M. and Sood, K. (2015) 'Why are there still so few men within early years in primary schools: Views from male trainee teachers and male leaders?', *Education 3–13*, 43(2), pp. 115–127.
Peeters, J., Rohrmann, T. and Emilsen, K. (2015) 'Gender balance in ECEC: Why is there so little progress?', *European Early Childhood Education Research Journal*, 23(3), pp. 302–314. doi: 10.1080/1350293X.2015.1043805.
Pre-school Learning Alliance (2011) *Parents "Want Men to Work as Childcarers in Day Nurseries"*. Available at: https://shop.pre-school.org.uk/media/press-releases/255/parents-want-men-to-work-as-childcarers-in-day-nurseries (accessed: 15th February 2019).
Read, J. (2003) 'Froebelian women: Networking to promote professional status and educational change in the nineteenth century', *History of Education*, 32(1), pp. 17–33. doi: 10.1080/0046760022000032396.
Rentzou, K. (2011) 'Greek parents' perceptions of male early childhood educators', *Early Years: An International Research Journal*, 31(2), pp. 135–147.
Roberts-Holmes, G. (2013) 'The English Early Years Professional Status (EYPS) and the 'split' Early Childhood Education and Care (ECEC) system', *European Early Childhood Education Research Journal*, 21(3), pp. 339–352. doi: 10.1080/1350293X.2012.704304.
Robinson, K.H. and Jones Diaz, C.J. (2016) *Diversity and Difference in Childhood: Issues for Theory and Practice*. London: Open University Press.
Rogoff, B. (1990) *Apprenticeship in Thinking: Cognitive Development in Social Context*. New York: Oxford University Press.
Skelton, C. (2012) 'Men teachers and the "feminised" primary school: A review of the literature', *Educational Review*, 64(1), pp. 1–19. doi: 10.1080/00131911.2011.616634.
Tovey, H. (2017) *Bringing the Froebel Approach to Your Early Years Practice*. Oxon: Routledge.

CHAPTER

6

What is the impact of the gender imbalance in the early years workforce?

Introduction

In the previous chapter we thought about why there is a gender imbalance in the early years workforce; now we are going to move on to consider the impact of this imbalance. Let us start by thinking about your own experiences. Did you attend an early years setting when you were young? Who do you remember working there? When we have spoken to school-aged children about their early years experiences, we've heard them talk about 'the ladies' who worked there, in settings predominantly staffed by female practitioners. If you went to an early years setting, we imagine your memories of the staff who worked there might be similar. Do you think that this might have influenced how you learnt, played and developed and if so, in what ways? Some of you will work in an early years setting with a predominantly female workforce. Do you think that the gender imbalance has an impact on how practitioners behave? We are going to consider all of these questions and ideas in this chapter by:

- building your understanding of the impact of this gender imbalance on children, the workforce and wider society,
- exploring some of the discussions around the specific contribution that male and female practitioners make,
- considering what a gender-flexible pedagogy would look like.

This chapter will consider whether male practitioners offer specific opportunities for children such as physical play, risky play and use of the outdoor environment (Emilsen and Koch, 2010; Sandseter, 2014; Van Polanen et al., 2017) or whether these suggestions are myths (Fatherhood Institute, 2017). It will question why some consider that female practitioners are not able to offer such a pedagogy, exploring the notion of 'gender-flexible' practitioners (Warin, 2017). At the same time, the chapter will highlight messages that may be communicated to children about appropriate cultural norms (Rogoff, 1990) by this lack of male practitioners.

Are there specific areas where male practitioners may be able to offer particular opportunities for children?

Some research studies suggest that male practitioners bring something different to their practice with young children compared to female practitioners (Josephidou, 2019). Therefore, the argument goes, an increase in the number of men in settings might positively influence the range of experiences for children. Three key areas of outdoor play, risky play and rough-and-tumble play have been specifically identified. Why men might have specialisms in these areas is open to interpretation – is it because of how they've been socialised, down to 'male' personality traits, or simply inherent? Let us now have a look at these three areas in turn.

Outdoor play

Within the EYFS there is the requirement that children have daily opportunities for outdoor play, unless circumstances like unsafe weather conditions make it unfeasible (Department for Education, 2017, p. 30). This echoes an international recognition of the importance of outdoor play in young children's learning. For instance, Bento and Dias (2017) identified three areas in particular where outdoor play can support children's development: by increasing contact with natural elements, opportunities to take risks and also opportunities for socialisation.

Some research suggests that male practitioners are more confident in the outdoor environment than in the traditional indoor environment. For example, Emilsen and Koch (2010) conducted a study in the Norwegian and Austrian context that explored how giving male practitioners more opportunities for outdoor play might be influential in increasing the number of men choosing to work in the Early Years. They cite Moss (2004, p. 2) who says that traditionally there is a view that 'workers with young children are substitute mothers, requiring only qualities and experiences assumed to be essentially female'. They give this as one of the reasons why men may not be attracted to a career in Early Years (along with status and pay) and suggest stereotypical male characteristics do not fit with the idea of being a 'substitute mother' working in a 'substitute home' (2010, p. 544). Thus, the outdoor environment may be one where men feel more suited because it does not have the same connotations of femininity as the indoor environment. In the Norwegian branch of their study they collected data from questionnaires completed by 121 male practitioners and 151 female practitioners and conducted interviews with ten men and four women working in outdoor preschools. They found that male practitioners who were allowed to stay outdoors felt 'more freedom to work with the children in their own way, without the tradition of caring being imposed on them' (p. 543), which thus may boost recruitment of men. Plus, the Norwegian participants said that men were more 'physical with children', 'playful with children' and 'less focused on safety and security' than women (2010, p. 548), which the participants viewed positively. This would support Bento and Dias's (2017) suggestion that outdoor play can support children's development by offering opportunities for socialisation and also for risky play.

Risky play

Other researchers have considered how the outdoor area is an ideal environment for a specific kind of play called 'risky play' (Sandseter, 2009). Positive risk-taking is an important part of children's lives: it develops their confidence, their thinking skills, creative skills, problem-solving skills and is vital for their well-being (Little et al., 2011; Madge and Barker, 2007; Sandseter, 2009; Stephenson, 2003). Some even go so far as to state that positive risk-taking is an essential part of being human and if we are not given the opportunity to do so we will look for it in other ways (Madge and Barker, 2007).

Like Emilsen and Koch (2010), Sandseter (2014) has explored how male practitioners may be able to offer a specific contribution to practice in risky play. She collected data from 116 practitioners in Norway (of whom 20% were male) to find out what their perceptions and practices are in relation to risky play. Her findings suggest that male practitioners 'have a more liberal attitude towards children's risky play, and allow children to engage in greater risky play than women' (p. 434), perhaps because they themselves enjoy risk-taking more. This is echoed by the London Early Years Foundation (LEYF, 2012) who cite research that men encourage children to take more risks and facilitate more physical and outdoor play (Fagan, 1996; Parke, 1996 and Lamb, 2000, cited in LEYF, 2012). However, Van Polanen et al. (2017) carried out observations on 42 practitioners of both sexes and did not find differences in how male and female practitioners gave attention to children, or the levels of sensitivity and stimulation they showed towards them. They hypothesise that part of the reason for the lack of differences may be down to the fact that as there is such a large gender imbalance in the early years workforce, 'male caregivers are exposed to a wide range of female-specific attitudes, behaviours and interactions' (2017: 421) which thus may affect how male practitioners act.

Rough-and-tumble play

Linked closely with the idea of risky play is the playful wrestling that children often engage in and is frequently described as rough-and-tumble play. Research tells us how important rough-and-tumble play is for young children (Bosacki et al., 2015; Tannock, 2008). It enables them to develop many skills such as self-control, self-regulation and spatial awareness. It is predominantly males (fathers or practitioners) that engage in this type of 'physically stimulating and unpredictable play' and in relation to parents, 'young children tend to select their fathers for play when they have a choice of partner' (Lewis and Lamb, 2003, p. 213).

This links to research conducted by Bretherton et al. (2005), in which they investigated how involved fathers see themselves. The majority of fathers saw themselves as 'a more active playmate' (2005; 245) than their child's mother in play activities including roughhousing, which they describe as 'horsing around, wrestling, rambunctious, and boisterous physical play' (p. 245). Similarly, the mothers interviewed in the study generally said that fathers engaged the child in this type of play more than them and were the more 'playful' parent. Some mothers and fathers linked this type of play to masculine characteristics and some talked about boisterous play as being 'a special aspect of the father-child relationship' (p. 245). We will consider more about the differences in how mothers and fathers may parent differently in Chapter 9 (Motherhood and fatherhood: Do parents engage with their children in gendered ways?). Similarly, in Sumsion's (2000a) research in the Australian context she found that male early childhood trainee teachers observed 'physical passivity, which the participants interpreted as a feminine preference' (p. 92). They noted that there was a lack of rough-and-tumble play, which they perceived as limiting children's opportunities for building relationships and not catering to boys' learning needs as much as girls'. We will come back to another piece of research by Sumsion (2000b) in a moment.

Although we believe there is evidence from research to support the idea that there are areas of provision where men can make a specific contribution to practice, the Fatherhood Institute (2017) has contested that assertion. They talk about how it is a common myth and stereotype that 'we need more men in ECE because men and women bring different skills to the table' (2017, p. 11). They suggest that there is little evidence that men are better at rough-and-tumble, outdoor and physical play and it is true that we don't know if they are *better* at doing it, however there are findings that suggest that men feel more comfortable in engaging in this type of play than women (Emilsen and Koch, 2010; Sandseter, 2014; Sumsion, 2000a). They also suggest that it would not be favourable to have a workforce solely of men or solely of women – we agree with this and with their suggestion that 'Surely the ideal scenario is a mixed gender workforce in which staff of both genders are fully competent and confident at the full range of activities and support from which children might benefit?' (2017, p. 11)

Time to consider

The stereotype that 'men and women bring different skills to the table' is just one of the myths that the Fatherhood Institute (2017, p. 9) say need contesting in relation to men working in early childhood. Below is the full list; think about what evidence you can find to challenge these beliefs:

1. Men are less suited to caring roles.
2. Men don't want to work in ECE because of low pay.
3. Recruiting men to work in ECE is social engineering.
4. Paedophiles are attracted to ECE and are mostly men.
5. We need more men in ECE because men and women bring different skills to the table … and because boys need role models.
6. Parents don't want men looking after their children.

If you want to read the Fatherhood Institute (2017) responses to these claims, you can access their report online:

Fatherhood Institute (2017) *How can we attract more men into London's early years workforce?* Available at: www.fatherhoodinstitute.org/wp-content/uploads/2017/09/MITEY-2017-London-report-1.pdf (accessed: 1st June 2019).

Is developing gender-flexible practice the way forward?

Let's consider the Fatherhood Institute (2017) statement that what would be most beneficial for early childhood settings is a mixed workforce of 'fully competent and confident' practitioners. We agree with them; if we focus too heavily on the idea that men should be leading on outdoor, rough-and-tumble and risky play in the early years setting, then there is the danger that negative stereotypes about 'what men do' and 'what women do' are being reinforced. A solution may be to develop a pedagogy where men and women are able to respond to the needs of children unconstrained by the stereotypes of their gender. Different researchers have coined different terms for this: Cushman (2005, p. 233) uses the term 'holistic approach', Sumsion (2000b, p. 134) refers to it as 'androgynous professional practice', while Warin (2017, p. 293) talks about the concept of 'gender flexibility'. Let us consider more fully definitions of these terms and what they could look like in practice.

A 'holistic approach' (Cushman, 2005)

While in other parts of the world the percentage of male early years practitioners has steadily increased, in New Zealand the opposite is true. Farquhar (2008, p. 734) notes how 'in 1992 around 2.34% of the childcare teaching workforce was male' yet by 2008 it had 'steadily slipped to just less than 1%'. In 2018 the figure is looking more positive, with men making up 3% of the early years workforce (Ministry of Education, 2019). The percentage of male primary school teachers is slightly higher at 16% (The World

Bank, 2019) yet this too is a figure that has dropped dramatically; in 1956, 42% of primary school teachers were male (Cushman, 2008). The decline in men in both workforces has been attributed to a highly publicised sexual abuse case involving a male ECEC practitioner and several female practitioners in the early 1990s; this had a huge impact on men's willingness to join the ECEC workforce because of the public's perception of male ECEC practitioners (Farquhar, 2008).

Cushman (2005) conducted a piece of research that explored male primary school teachers' views on why they joined the profession, issues of status, pay and other challenges. Participants talked about how their gender may have helped them secure employment, because of 'the public demand for more male role models' (Cushman, 2005, p. 232) which are, Cushman argues, often seen to be beneficial for those without a father figure at home – something we will discuss more in Chapter 9 (Motherhood and fatherhood: Do parents engage with their children in gendered ways?). Because the participants in Cushman's research knew they were seen as role models, they knew that they had to think carefully about how they were portraying men. One participant used the term 'holistic approach' to describe how he aimed for his teaching style to echo his belief that 'masculine and feminine traits are not the sole prerogative of the respective gender' (p. 233) – essentially demonstrating a gender-flexible way of teaching.

'Androgynous professional practice' (Sumsion, 2000b)

Sumsion (2000b) conducted a piece of research in which she carried out two in-depth interviews and several conversations with one male preschool teacher, Bill, in the Australian context. She wanted to gather his perspectives on how he positioned himself in respect to his gender and also how he believed he was positioned by others. He aimed to challenge assumptions that he would have different practices to his female colleagues as a result of his gender. Sumsion (2000b, p. 134) quotes Bill as saying 'I am just one of the team' and that 'we all do things very similarly', which she describes as him 'presenting an image of androgynous professional practice'. Essentially, Bill aims to minimise any conceivable differences between him and his co-workers, perhaps in part because he wants to avoid the risk of any allegations of abuse on the grounds of his gender. The *Oxford English Dictionary* explains that originally the term 'androgynous' had negative connotations, describing a man who was effeminate or feminine characteristics, although it now says that it is usually used in a positive or neutral sense to mean 'a person who is neither clearly male nor clearly female, or who combines elements of masculinity and femininity' (*OED*, 2019). However, not everyone thinks that 'androgynous' is the best word to use in this context.

'Gender flexibility' (Warin, 2017)

The concept of 'androgyny' can be problematic because it's still suggesting that there are typically masculine and feminine traits and characteristics. Warin (2017) thinks this term is unhelpful because it is still 'essentialist'; that is to say it is suggesting that 'this is what males do and this is what females do so let's mix it all together'. This is why she prefers the term 'gender-flexible' to describe what she thinks best practice is with regard to male and female practitioners' behaviours. Fundamentally it means acting in a way that responds to the needs of the children regardless of practitioner gender. She says the term contrasts with the idea of 'gender balance'; instead of aiming for a balance in male and female practitioners, Warin argues, ECEC settings should aim for 'gender flexibility', which she describes as incorporating 'ideas about the resources and activities that young children themselves may be encouraged to engage in, with an emphasis on playful and experimental approaches to the performance of gender' (2017, p. 2). So rather than early years settings needing to change in respect to the number of male practitioners they employ, Warin is suggesting that the change they need to make is with regard to staff not being constrained by the stereotypes of their gender.

Time to consider

Warin (2017) talks about gender-flexible practice but what would this kind of practice look like? Make a list of things that are effective practice in terms of working with young children. Then think about who can do these – men, women or both? Here are some ideas to start you off:

- stimulating activities,
- providing challenge,
- warm relationships,
- working with parents,
- knowledge and understanding of how children develop.

What do children think of the gender imbalance?

So far in this chapter we have considered two big ideas. Firstly, whether there are areas of practice where male practitioners might make a specific contribution. Secondly, whether we should be moving away from the idea of a gender-balanced workforce towards one of gender-flexible practitioners. Whichever approach you might currently be in favour of, we believe that the current gender imbalance and inflexibility is having an impact on children.

We think it is important to consider what children think of the current imbalance and how it might have an impact on their understanding cultural norms (Rogoff, 1990).

Children's perspectives on the gender imbalance

There is a real lack of literature which examines children's perspectives on the gender imbalance in the early years workforce (Harty, 2007; Harris and Barnes, 2009). Harty (2007) suggests a solution to the lack of children's opinions would be to include the voice of the child much more in this kind of research. Harris and Barnes (2009), when they carried out their research in the Australian context into young children's perceptions of practitioner gender perspectives, also recognised that there was already little work in this area. Although there is a growing interest in male practitioners, their experiences and their unique contribution, there is a gap in the literature in terms of children's voices. So, along with a colleague, we conducted a small-scale study to explore children's perspectives (Bolshaw et al., 2017). From a previous piece of research we had conducted with male Early Childhood Studies students, we knew that they were never offered opportunities as male pupils to engage in work-based experiences which would have developed their understanding of working with young children (Josephidou et al., 2016).

We were interested to find out at what age and at what stage in their educational journey children might come to the realisation that a career in ECEC is 'women's work', so we posed the research question: 'How do children express their perceptions of the early years workforce in relation to gender?' and conducted group interviews with children ranging from four to eleven years old. We chose group interviews in an attempt to make children feel the most comfortable taking part. Group interviews also have the advantage, Einarsdottir (2007, p. 200) suggests, of allowing children 'to help each other with the answers, remind each other about details, and keep the answers truthful'.

For the children aged between seven and eleven, we began the interviews by inviting children to share their experiences of their early years settings. We then used photo elicitation, by introducing photographs taken in other early years settings, for the children to handle, pass to each other and talk about. We spoke to the children about what they could see in the photos generally and then spoke about how the photographs featured both men and women working with young children. We explored whether the children thought it important that there are both men and women working in nurseries, whether they thought men and women who work in nurseries do the same jobs, and whether they thought they act and behave in the same way or in different ways. Questions then moved towards asking children whether they thought that they would like to work in a nursery or preschool, and why, and what kind of people they thought would be good at working in nurseries and preschools.

When interviewing the four- to six-year-olds we used the 'teddy interviewer' technique (O'Reilly and Dogra, 2017; Roberts-Holmes, 2011). O'Reilly and Dogra (2017, p. 126) suggest that teddies might be useful to explore how children feel about certain issues, as they give children the permission to say what they think. Roberts-Holmes (2011, p. 158) also suggests that soft toys can be an effective way for researchers to engage in child-centred discussions with children, as this helps to minimise 'the high-control, adult-dominated and question and answer format' (Brooker, 2011, p. 166, cited in Roberts-Holmes, 2011) that interviews have the possibility of becoming. So in our interviews with the younger children we introduced 'Teddy' and gave the children background information that he was nearly due to start preschool and so had been visiting lots of settings. We explained that he was confused because he didn't see any men working there and so could the children please explain to him what happens in early years settings.

Both interview techniques gave us some valuable data about children's perspectives on the lack of men working in ECEC. We found that there were differences according to the children's age, as Table 6.1 shows.

When asked whether it was important that there were both men and women working in ECEC settings, two of the older participants responded as follows:

'I think it might be very important because girls should have everything to work and do whatever they want and be whatever they want and the boys too, so I think everybody should, be able to, if they want to, do everything they want to, to vote, everyone should be able to'

'Well it's not really about whether you are male or female, but like skin colour, it doesn't really matter what skin colour you have to be at a nursery or even to go to a nursery.'

TABLE 6.1 Showing children's perspectives on the gender imbalance in the ECEC workforce

Ages 4–6	• One participant spoke about how ECE settings were 'just too full of ladies' for any man to be able to work there. • This was because 'more ladies like children' and they were better at helping children than men. • In any case the men needed to work, either 'with older children', 'building houses', 'with computers because they are better than ladies' at this, or 'in London nearly the whole day, usually in the office' as their fathers did.

Ages 7–11	• For these children, it was because 'women have babies and look after them', that 'normally most women like to deal with kids and when you walk around, there are just more women with kids than men'. Another participant added that 'women like to stay at home and look after their own children'.
	• When asked why men might not want to work in the ECEC workforce, these children were able to come up with some good theories as to why this might be the case. Participants suggested:
	  • 'Maybe the men think that it's a sissy job, just for ladies'
	  • 'Maybe because their friends have said something … or something is on the internet or something like that, or on Facebook or something'
	  • 'Because like, maybe they wouldn't, they would think they would get like second thoughts about being in a playgroup or being a teacher, but they should just be encouraged'.

Our research showed that children do recognise that there is a gender imbalance in the workforce and that they are able to suppose some reasons why this might be the case. Importantly, the older children were able to articulate that men should be encouraged to consider a career in the ECEC workforce. It is significant that we know that at a young age, children are not averse to the idea that men should work with young children. Perhaps we need to think more about why, when making career choices, more men are not considering a career in ECEC.

The impact on cultural norms (Rogoff, 1990)

One reason that might explain why men are not considering a career in ECEC is because of how cultural norms are transmitted to children. A gender imbalance in the workforce may be implicitly communicating to children that the ECEC workforce is not for men. This links to a concept that Rogoff (1990) has proposed, that of *guided participation*.

Theorist in focus: Rogoff's (1990) theory of guided participation

Barbara Rogoff is a researcher whose ideas have been informed by Vygotsky's theories of the zone of proximal development (ZPD). She coined the idea of *guided participation*, which is like Vygotsky's theory of ZPD in the sense that she acknowledges that adults play an important role in the development of children through how they step in when appropriate to scaffold children's learning. It has been described as:

> Guided participation stresses tacit forms of communication in the verbal and non-verbal exchanges of daily life and the distal arrangements involved in the regulation of children's activities, material goods, and companions. The notion of guided participation emphasizes the active role of children in both observing and participating in the organized societal activity of their caregivers and companions. In this more inclusive approach, the aim is to encompass more of the daily activities in which children participate and develop skill in and understanding of the valued approaches of their cultural community.
>
> (Rogoff et al., 1998, p. 229)

We know that the quotation above may be tricky to understand, so it's worth having a careful read over it and using a dictionary if necessary (we admit we hadn't come across the word 'distal' before). If you do study it closely, you might agree with us that a key word in the quotation above is the word 'tacit'. It means 'something that is understood even though it has not been expressed explicitly'. Without openly saying it, young children may be guided in their thinking to understand that the early years workforce is not a place for men, because of what they observe there and who they see participating in those settings as part of their daily activities. The cultural norm that may be transmitted to children is that it is women, not men, who participate in the 'organized societal activity' of working in ECEC. Moreover, it is important to note that in guided participation the 'active role' of children is acknowledged, meaning that children are able to influence gender roles too, based upon what they are observing.

So, when considering the impact that a gender imbalance may be having on children it is important to bear Rogoff's (1990) idea of guided participation in mind. It reminds us that we need to think not only about how a lack of men in the workforce may be influencing the kind of practice that children experience in their early years settings, but also the implicit lessons they are learning about 'what men do' and 'what women do', which will impact on wider society as they grow older, particularly as children are *actively* participating and potentially influencing gender roles. Not to mention that the imbalance may impact on their career aspirations, too.

Case study

Nerice is an early years practitioner in a packaway setting. A researcher has asked to interview her about the need for male practitioners. She considers what they might bring to a setting and questions whether this means that what she provides is not good enough. What arguments would you use to convince her that more men are needed to work with young children? Then consider the opposite argument. Why is trying to recruit more men into the early years workforce problematic?

Possible response

You could organise your answers into a for-and-against debate. We have started to do this for you in Table 6.2; see if you can complete it.

Final reflection

In this chapter we have thought about the impact of the gender imbalance in the early years workforce. We have considered how some areas of provision – like outdoor play, risky play and rough-and-tumble play – might be areas where men can make a specific contribution. We've thought about whether there's

TABLE 6.2 Debating whether more men are needed in the early years workforce

Debate: More men are needed in the early years workforce	
For	Against
Children could have more opportunities to engage in risky play.	If men joined the early years workforce and then behave in gendered ways gender stereotypes will be reinforced for young children

evidence that men and women bring different attributes to practice and why it is important that practitioners are 'gender-flexible'. We have also thought about how the gender imbalance in the workforce may impact on how young children perceive a career in early childhood.

Key points

- There might be areas where men can make a specific contribution to practice in ECEC – particularly with regard to children's outdoor play, risky play and rough-and-tumble play. These are areas which may be seen as less feminised and where men may feel more comfortable taking a lead.
- Different researchers have used different terms to describe how practitioners could adapt their practices to remove the stereotypes of which characteristics men and women typically display. Cushman (2005) refers to this as taking 'a holistic approach', Sumsion, 2000b) refers to it as the 'androgynous professional' while Warin (2017) advocates 'gender-flexible practice'.
- Children are able to surmise some reasons for the gender imbalance in the workforce yet believe men should be encouraged to join the field. The imbalance may have an impact on their development of cultural norms and of their career aspirations, which strengthens the reasons why the imbalance should be addressed.

Further reading

1. Emilsen, K. and Koch, B. (2010) 'Men and women in outdoor play – Changing the concepts of caring findings from Norwegian and Austrian research projects', *European Early Childhood Education Research Journal*, 18(4), pp. 543–553.

   Have a look at Emilsen and Koch's (2010) study that explored male and female practitioners' views on outdoor play in Austrian and Norway and how increasing outdoor play in settings may attract more men to work in the early childhood sector.

2. Warin, J. and Gannerud, E. (2014) 'Gender, teaching and care: A comparative global conversation'. *Gender and Education*, 26(3), pp. 193–199.

   In 2014, a special edition of the journal *Gender and Education* was written (volume 3), which you might find useful as it examines the 'intersection of care and teaching practices within educational contexts'. Have a look at Warin and Gannerud's (2014) article in particular. They recognise that the concept of care is not easy to define but that it does carry with it many assumptions such as it is something that females do much better or that care comes naturally to females. They also argue that 'a re-conceptualisation of what care is is needed to begin to loosen the links between care, femininity and women's work'.

References

Bento, G. and Dias, G. (2017) 'The importance of outdoor play for young children's healthy development', *Porto Biomedical Journal*, 2(5), pp. 157–160.

Bolshaw, P., Josephidou, J. and O'Connor, S. (2017) *Exploring children's perceptions of the gendered nature of the early years workforce.* 69th Annual OMEP World Conference. Conference Centre Tamaris, Opatija, pp. 20–24 June.

Bosacki, S., Woods, H. and Coplan, R. (2015) 'Canadian female and male early childhood educators' perceptions of child aggression and rough-and-tumble play', *Early Child Development and Care*, 185(7), pp. 1134–1147. doi: 10.1080/03004430.2014.980408

Bretherton, I., Lambert, J.D. and Golby, B. (2005) 'Involved fathers of preschool children as seen by themselves and their wives: Accounts of attachment, socialization, and companionship', *Attachment & Human Development*, 7(3), pp. 229–251. doi: 10.1080/14616730500138341

Cushman, P. (2005) 'Let's hear it from the males: Issues facing male primary school teachers', *Teaching and Teacher Education*, 21(3), pp. 227–240.

Cushman, P. (2008) 'So what exactly do you want? What principals mean when they say 'male role model', *Gender and Education*, 20(2), pp. 123–136.

Department for Education (2017) *Statutory framework for the early years foundation stage.* Available at: www.foundationyears.org.uk/files/2017/03/EYFS_STATUTORY_FRAMEWORK_2017.pdf (accessed: 23rd August 2019).

Einarsdottir, J. (2007) 'Research with children: Methodological and ethical challenges', *European Early Childhood Education Research Journal*, 15(2), pp. 197–211.

Emilsen, K. and Koch, B. (2010) 'Men and women in outdoor play— Changing the concepts of caring findings from Norwegian and Austrian research projects', *European Early Childhood Education Research Journal*, 18(4), pp. 543–553.

Farquhar, S. (2008) 'New Zealand men's participation in early years work', *Early Child Development and Care*, 178(7-8), pp. 733–744.

Fatherhood Institute (2017) *How Can We Attract More Men into London's Early Years Workforce?* Available at: www.fatherhoodinstitute.org/wp-content/uploads/2017/09/MITEY-2017-London-report-1.pdf (accessed: 23rd August 2019).

Harris, K. and Barnes, S. (2009) 'Male teacher, female teacher: Exploring children's perspectives of teachers' roles in kindergartens', *Early Child Development and Care*, 179(2), pp. 167–181.

Harty, R. (2007) 'The men as role models argument: A case for researching children's views', *New Zealand Research in Early Childhood Education Journal*, 10, pp. 183–190.

Josephidou, J. (2019) 'A gendered contribution to play? Perceptions of Early Childhood Education and Care (ECEC) practitioners in England on how their gender influences their approaches to play', *Early Years*, doi: 10.1080/09575146.2019.1655713

Josephidou, J., Bolshaw, P. and O'Connor, S. (2016) *Exploring Male Early Childhood studies students' perceptions of working with young children in terms of a viable career choice.* OMEP European Conference 2016, 7th May 2016, Canterbury, Christ Church University.

Little, H., Wyver, S. and Gibson, F. (2011) 'The influence of play context and adult attitudes on young children's physical risk-taking during outdoor play', *European Early Childhood Education Research Journal*, 19(1), pp. 113–131.

London Early Years Foundation (2012) *Men working in childcare: Does it matter to children? What do they say?* Available at: www.leyf.org.uk/wp-content/uploads/2018/06/Men-in-Childcare-Version-141112.pdf (accessed: 31st May 2019).

Madge, N. and Barker, J. (2007) *Risk & Childhood*. London: Royal Society for the encouragement of Arts, Manufactures & Commerce.

Ministry of Education (2019) *Overview of ECE Teaching Staff in 2018*. Available at: www.educationcounts.govt.nz/__data/assets/pdf_file/0011/192944/ECE-Summary-page-3Teaching-staff-in-2018.pdf (accessed: 6th August 2019).

Moss, P. (2004) 'The early childhood workforce', In *'Developed Countries': Basic Structures and Education, UNESCO Policy Brief on Early Childhood*, Nr. 27, October 2004.

O'Reilly, M. and Dogra, N. (2017) *Interviewing Children and Young People for Research*. London: Sage.

OED Online (2019) 'androgynous, adj.' Available at: www.oed.com/view/Entry/7331?rskey=kDyRkX&result=1&isAdvanc ed=false (accessed: November 20, 2019).

Roberts-Holmes, G. (2011) *Doing your Early Years Research Project: A Step by Step Guide*. London: Sage.

Rogoff, B. (1990) *Apprenticeship in Thinking: Cognitive Development in Social Context*. New York: Oxford University Press.

Rogoff, B., Mistry, J., Göncü, A. and Mosier, C. (1998) 'Toddlers' guided participation with their caregivers in cultural activity', in: M. Woodhead, D. Faulkner and K. Littleton (eds) *Cultural Worlds of Early Childhood*. London: Routledge, pp. 225–249.

Sandseter, E. (2009) 'Children's expressions of exhilaration and fear in risky play', *Contemporary Issues in Early Childhood*, 10(2), pp. 92–106.

Sandseter, E. (2014) 'Early childhood education and carepractitioners' perceptions of children's risky play. Examining the influence of personality and gender', *Early Child Development and Care*, 184(3), pp. 434–449.

Stephenson, A. (2003) 'Physical Risk-taking: Dangerous or endangered?', *Early Years*, 23(1), pp. 35–43. doi: 10.1080/0957514032000045573

Sumsion, J. (2000a) 'Rewards, risks and tensions: Perceptions of males enrolled in an early childhood teacher education programme', *Asia-Pacific Journal of Teacher Education*, 28(1), pp. 87–100. doi: 10.1080/135986600109462

Sumsion, J. (2000b) 'Negotiating otherness: A male early childhood educator's gender positioning', *International Journal of Early Years Education*, 8(2), pp. 129–140. doi:10.1080/09669760050046174

Tannock, M.T. (2008) 'Rough and tumble play: An investigation of the perceptions of educators and young children', *Early Childhood Education Journal*, 35(4), pp. 357–361. doi: 10.1007/s10643-007-0196-1

Van Polanen, M., Colonnesi, C., Tavecchio, L.W.C., Blokhuis, S. and Fukkink, R.G. (2017) 'Men and women in childcare: A study of caregiver–child interactions', *European Early Childhood Education Research Journal*, 25(3), pp. 412–424.

Warin, J. (2017) 'Conceptualising the value of male practitioners in early childhood education and care: gender balance or gender flexibility', *Gender and Education*, 31(3), pp. 293–308.

The World Bank (2019) *Primary education, teachers (% female) New Zealand*. Available at: https://data.worldbank.org/indicator/SE.PRM.TCHR.FE.ZS?locations=NZ (accessed: 6th August 2019).

CHAPTER

7

How can we achieve a more gender-balanced workforce?

Introduction

Think about the men in your life –whether family, friends or colleagues. We imagine that the majority of them are not already members of the early years workforce. Now think about one in particular that you believe might have the right qualities and characteristics for an ECEC practitioner. Do you think he would be interested in working in early childhood? If not, why not? And do you think there are any initiatives that might encourage him to consider a career working with young children? We will think about what initiatives might work in this chapter; look at what has already been tried both in the UK and abroad; and what could be attempted in the future to make a career in the ECEC more appealing to men. This chapter will:

- consider ways that the gender imbalance in the workforce can be addressed,
- critique initiatives that have been used nationally and internationally to address the imbalance,
- consider the positive outcomes of a gender-balanced workforce.

In this chapter we will set out the positive impact of having a greater percentage than 2% (Brody, 2014) of men in the early years workforce and how children, the workforce and wider society could benefit. We will consider initiatives that have focused on attracting more men and consider how successful, and also how inclusive, they have been. We will reflect on the notion that, although there has been a movement of women into traditionally male workplaces, there has been limited movement in the opposite direction. We will also compare the early years workforce with other traditionally gendered workforces, such as nursing, to see if parallels can be drawn.

What initiatives are taking place in the UK to address the imbalance?

You will remember back in Chapter 5 (Why is there a gender imbalance in the early years workforce?) we considered where England's Department for Education policy had expressed a desire for more male ECEC practitioners. It is pertinent to think about what actions have been taken, or are being taken, to support those policies. It has been said that the workforce over-relies 'on young white women' (Rolfe, 2006, p. 103) and has been described as a 'gender ghetto' (Equal Opportunities Commission, 2003, p. 3). But what is happening to change this? We are going to start by thinking about the initiatives taking place in the UK and then in the next section we will look at what's happening elsewhere.

GenderEYE

In Chapter 5 we mentioned the 2017 Early Years Workforce Strategy (Department for Education, 2017a) and how it states that 'encouraging increased gender diversity among those joining the early years sector would have two main benefits; an increased pool of applicants for the sector to recruit from and male role models for young children' (p. 24). You might be wondering what happened as a result of that strategy. The report stated that to address the barrier of the recruitment and retention of male practitioners, the DfE would 'set up a 'task and finish group' of early years sector stakeholders to consider gender diversity in the sector in more depth' (2017, p. 25). This group was chaired by David Wright, owner of Paintpots Nurseries in Southampton and chair of the Southampton Men in Early Years group, with the Fatherhood Institute's Dr Jeremy Davies as deputy chair. The task and finish group delivered their report to the DfE in 2018 and, as a result, the DfE decided to invest £30,000 in a project which aims to challenge the stereotypes that exist in relation to the role that men can play in ECEC (Department for Education, 2019). The project is being jointly delivered by the Fatherhood Institute and Lancaster University under the name GenderEYE.

The GenderEYE project has four main aims, which are:

1 to explore the extent and nature of efforts to recruit and support male practitioners and their impact,

2 to consider how the value of men's presence is attributed and what theories (explicit and implicit) are articulated to support, refute or undermine (consciously or otherwise) the recruitment of men,

3 to identify barriers to male recruitment; map men's routes into ECE; understand their motivations and strategies they may have used, if required, to overcome barriers; and identify what support is needed to enable male employees to flourish and remain in the ECE profession,

4   based on the evidence above, to develop a workable and explicit theoretical framework to rationalise the value of including men within the ECE workforce; and create accessible training and resources to support and strengthen efforts to make the sector more gender-diverse and gender-sensitive.

To do this, the researchers are using several data collection methods. To start, they are gathering the perspectives of ECEC practitioners and managers about aspects of their roles via online surveys. This includes, in the practitioner survey, questions about the extent to which the participant would find it useful to have: (a) gender related training, (b) discussions of gendered experiences in supervisions and (c) informal chats among colleagues about gender. The survey also asks practitioners whether they believe the extent to which they are asked to do tasks (such as nappy changing, lifting items, cleaning, comforting children and tracking learning) is influenced by their gender.

Time to consider

Take a moment to think about how you would answer the following questions:

- Do you think you'd benefit from any of the interventions that the survey proposes?
- If you've worked in an ECEC setting, do you think your tasks at work have been affected by your gender?
- Now think about if you were conducting this research – what questions would you want to ask managers that might help you better understand what might support the recruitment of male practitioners?

The project is also going to work with partners in Norway to attempt to learn about what is happening in Norway and to explain their higher percentage of male practitioners, which currently stands at 10.3% (Statistics Norway, 2019). It will consider the steps they are taking to meet the Norwegian government's target of 20% male practitioners by 2020. The researchers will conduct case studies in preschool centres and conduct interviews with 'key training providers, careers stakeholders and key early years strategists' (GenderEYE, 2019) too. One thing that is possibly lacking is the child's voice in this research, particularly considering what we said in Chapter 6 (What is the impact of the gender imbalance in the early years workforce?). But this is something that the London Early Years Foundation (LEYF) have considered in their recent research, which we will talk about in a moment.

The Department for Education (2019) has stated that the GenderEYE project should lead to an 'innovative recruitment drive' to help both ECEC employers and careers advisors be able to publicise the important roles that men can play in ECEC. They state that the project should also lead to the creation of 'practical resources like mythbusters, "how-to" guides and online content to support male recruitment into the profession, as well as online peer support for men already working in the sector'. The idea of peer support for current male practitioners is an important one; Warin (2018) suggests that there is a value in male-only support groups and mentoring, for instance because they can provide emotional support. However, she does express some disadvantages with them as they may 'exacerbate binary thinking and entrench the very differences they are hoping to overcome' (p. 132). This is why she agrees with the European Early Childhood Education and Care (ECEC) gender researchers (2016) that both single-sex and mixed-sex groups are beneficial for gender-sensitisation training.

MITEY

Although the GenderEYE project aims to increase the use of peer-support networks for men already working in ECEC; in the UK some of these do exist, both on local and national levels, in the form of Men In The Early Years (MITEY). This is a campaign run by the Fatherhood Institute to support men who work, or who are considering working, in ECEC. The five statements which make up their charter are:

- We value men's capacity to care for and educate children, both within families and as professionals
- We value the benefits to children of being educated and cared for by a diverse, mixed-gender early years workforce
- We acknowledge that early years education should benefit from the talents of all, so we are actively seeking to create a workforce that includes men, women and people with other gendered or non-gendered identities
- We are committed to removing the obstacles that stand in the way of a mixed-gender early years workforce, including low pay and status, limited career progression and gender-discriminatory treatment
- We view early years education as a critical context in which to address gender inequality and stereotypes, for the benefit of children and wider society.

(MITEY, 2019)

Yet 'actively seeking to create a workforce that includes men, women and people with other gendered or non-gendered identities' can be harder than it appears. Targeting males in recruitment initiatives is a strategy that has been undertaken with little success previously in both England and internationally (Oberhuemer, 2011). Just as recruiting men is not a simple exercise, neither is supporting men in completing any specific study programme and then encouraging them to stay in the profession (Thornton and Bricheno, 2006). This is why peer-support groups are important; they can provide support to men both as they enter the profession and remain within it.

Time to consider

Take a moment to reflect on the five statements that make up the MITEY charter. Do you agree with them? If not, which ones would you challenge? Do you think other people might challenge some of these statements? If you think they might, then that might explain why the ECEC field has some way to go before the number of male practitioners in the sector increases. And, finally, if you were to write your own charter to support a more gender-balanced or gender-flexible workforce, what would it look it?

The London Early Years Foundation

Other organisations, too, are taking steps to develop the gender balance. One of these is the London Early Years Foundation (LEYF). In 2019 the CEO, June O'Sullivan MBE, stated that 'we need to have a diverse workforce with a variety of interaction styles, interests and approaches to teaching, regardless of gender. It should be about who teaches the activity the best' (Perkins et al., 2019, p. 3). Does this perspective ring any bells with you? If you think back to Chapter 6 (What is the impact of the gender imbalance in the early years workforce?) then O'Sullivan's sentiment might remind you of what Warin (2017) calls 'gender flexibility', Sumsion (2000) calls 'androgynous professional practice' and Cushman (2005) refers to as 'the holistic approach'. To make the workforce more diverse, with respect to gender, O'Sullivan pledges that LEYF will do four important things:

1. continue to garner widespread support (and acceptance) for men working in childcare across the early years sector among peers and parents,
2. recruit early years male role models as ambassadors to schools, colleges and career fairs etc.,
3. develop a national Men in Early Years Advisory Group to meet twice a year to assess and monitor progress,
4. create a professional development programme to recognise and support personal contribution from employees, regardless of gender.

Men in Childcare charity

And it's not just in England that initiatives are being supported by government funds. In Scotland, the Men in Childcare charity has received Scottish government funding since 2006. Since 2001, the charity, which also receives funding from the City of Edinburgh Council, has offered free evening courses to men wishing to work in ECEC. And since 2005, over a thousand men have enrolled on their courses which focus on children's development and learning (Scottish Government, 2018a). This may explain why the percentage of male ECEC practitioners in Scotland stands at 4% (Scottish Government, 2018b), being slightly higher than 2% in the UK as a whole. Hansen et al. (2006, cited in Cameron, 2006) describe how fully funded men-only training programmes have had a positive effect in attracting men to consider a career in early childhood.

And the initiatives in Scotland don't stop there. In October 2018, the Scottish government pledged a further £50,000 to create a Men in Early Years Challenge Fund with the aim of increasing the number of men who enrol in ECEC studies. Part of the fund was given to the University of the Highlands and Islands (UHI), which has now also begun delivering men-only evening classes to males considering a career in ECEC. Yet, it is important to note that the desire to increase the number of men working in ECEC is not solely to create gender balance, it is also because there is a current shortfall in the number of ECEC practitioners in Scotland (TheyWorkForYou, 2019); an extra 11,000 are needed as the number of funded hours offered by the government has increased (Wane, 2019).

What initiatives are taking place outside the UK to address the imbalance?

It's important, too, to look at what interventions are happening outside of the UK to attract men to careers in ECEC. Back in 1996, the European Commission Childcare Network set a target that 20% of staff working in ECEC settings should be male by 2006, which would help to challenge gender stereotypes and increase the involvement of fathers (1996, p. 30). Then, in 2001, the OECD's first 'Starting strong' report argued that 'there is a critical need to develop strategies to recruit and retain a qualified and diverse, mixed-gender workforce' (OECD, 2001, p. 11). Ten years later, the European Commission (2011) stated:

> There is a very important issue of gender balance among ECEC staff. Almost all of them are women. This has been a matter of concern for a long time. A few countries have set targets for the recruitment of men into ECEC or sought to redesign the profession to reduce gendering. There is a pressing need to make a career in the ECEC sector more attractive to men in all EU countries.

As we have seen, the issue of recruiting more men to ECEC is an international, long-standing one; it is therefore useful to look at the strategies that have been used by other countries to add a greater degree of gender balance to the workforce. Many places are thinking carefully about how to recruit more men, including Norway and Sweden.

Norway

As we said earlier, in Norway currently 10.3% of the ECEC workforce is male (Statistics Norway, 2019). This is impressive, although a long way off the target of 20% by 2020 which the Norwegian government set back in 2011 (Norwegian Ministry of Children, Equality and Social Inclusion, 2011, p. 19). Because of Norway's success, many researchers including Brody (2014) and Peeters et al. (2015) have examined what it is that Norway is doing to increase the number of male practitioners.

Peeters et al. (2015) have explored Norway's attempts to increase the participation of men in the ECEC workforce in a journal article that also considers recruitment attempts in Belgium and Germany. Their article states that government attempts to recruit male practitioners have been in force since 2001 in a series of Governmental Action Plans for Gender Equality. They go on to explain that, as part of these action plans, Networks for Men in Kindergartens (MIB) was established as a way of supporting men to remain in the ECEC workforce and to support the recruitment of new male practitioners. You might be reminded of the MITEY group we spoke about earlier and the plans within the new GenderEYE project to create support networks for male practitioners too.

In Brody's (2014) research he looked at six men from six different cultures, one of whom, Reidar Eliassen, lives in Norway. Reidar is a pedagogic leader at an ECEC setting, in Oslo, which is part of a chain that has a 22% male workforce. Reidar's mentor, Oivind Hornslien, director of one of the other settings in the chain, talks about how he follows 'a national policy that permits him to take affirmative action towards men applying for what is traditionally a women's job' (p. 111). What that means is that when he is advertising a post, all the male job applicants are automatically offered an interview. Brody also cites research by Menka-Eide (2012, cited in Brody, 2014), who compares Norway to New Zealand – both countries were hit by a child-abuse scandal in 1993. (We discussed the case of New Zealand back in Chapter 6.) While the New Zealand government took no action to challenge perceptions about men working in ECEC, Norway instead decided to attract men to the workforce and promote the benefits of male practitioners to the public; this may in part explain why Norway leads the way in aiming for a gender-balanced workforce.

Reidar's job title of 'pedagogic leader' is not one that is often used in ECEC, however Rolfe (2005) suggests that the term, and what it implies about the role of the ECEC practitioner, might play a role in attracting men to the workforce in Norway. She suggests (although bear in mind that Rolfe published her thoughts back in 2005) that working in ECEC is different in some other European countries to the UK (particularly Denmark and Norway), because it is 'more knowledge-based and educational' (p. 6), which would thus reflect the 'pedagogic leader' term. This term, and the perceived difference in the role of the ECEC practitioner, may give childcare a higher status in Norway and thus have a greater degree of appeal to men.

And finally, Norway also has a scheme, known as the Lillehammer Model, which aims to encourage men to consider careers in ECEC (The Royal Ministry of Children, Equality and Social Inclusion, 2015, p. 22). Boys in lower secondary school are given the opportunity to complete work experience in childcare settings to support play activities. The aim is to showcase and share information about what a career in ECEC could look like. We know this is something we need to consider internationally; remember the OECD (2015) report 'The ABC of gender equality in education' which we have already mentioned several times in this book? Part of the report considers the expectations and realities for those leaving school across the world, in terms of their career choices. Their research has found that 'Pre-primary education teaching professional', 'Pre-primary education teaching associate professional' and 'Childcare worker' were listed as girls' top-ten career choices in several OECD countries, yet none of these professions made the boys' top-ten lists in any countries.

In the same report, 'medical doctor' was listed as a top-ten profession by both girls and boys (in 32 OECD countries and 26 OECD countries respectively). Yet although 'nursing and midwifery professional' made the girls' top-ten list in 13 OECD countries, those professions did not make the top-ten boys' list in any country. This is something important to acknowledge – the differing career aspirations between boys and girls have an impact on gender imbalance in other workforces too. Warin (2018) talks about how we may be able to learn from professions such as nursing and adult social care, which traditionally also have a low percentage of male workers. She cites Williams (2017), whose findings suggest there are similarities to explain the lack of men in both the nursing and ECEC sectors – 'a lack of career advice and the need for male-inclusive forms of training and gender-awareness training to overcome traditional hegemonic masculinity stereotypes' (Warin, 2017, p. 127). But perhaps this is a sector where Norway isn't leading the way – in both Norway and the UK the percentage of the nursing and midwifery workforce stands at 11% (NMC, 2018; Statistics Norway, 2018).

Sweden

When thinking about how to develop the number of male practitioners in the long term, an interesting country to consider is Sweden. Currently the percentage of male practitioners stands at 5% (Swedish Institute, 2019), which is similar to that of the UK's 2%. But unlike the UK, Sweden has a much longer history of attempting to recruit men to the ECEC workforce. Hedlin et al. (2018) report that in the 1970s male applicants to preschool teacher education were prioritised as part of a scheme to have a certain quota of male students. However, what is interesting about Sweden now is how they are trying to influence boys' decisions to consider a career in ECEC in the long term.

You will certainly be familiar with the Early Years Foundation Stage (Department for Education, 2017b), the framework that guides learning and development children between birth and five in ECEC settings in England. The Swedish equivalent is called the 'Curriculum for the preschool' and it sets out what the fundamental values for preschools should be and what preschools, staff teams and managers should be doing to support children's development. One of the fundamental values is around Equitable Education. Within that section it states:

> The preschool should actively and consciously promote the equal rights and opportunities of all children, regardless of gender. The preschool also has a responsibility to combat gender patterns that limit children's development, choices and learning. How the preschool organises education, how children are treated and what demands and expectations are made of children all contribute to shaping their perceptions of what is female and what is male. The preschool should therefore organise education so that children mix, play and learn together, and test and develop their abilities and interests, with the same opportunities and on equal terms, regardless of gender.
> Swedish National Agency for Education (2018, p. 8)

The curriculum goes on to include several more statements about gender, including the requirement that the work team in a setting should 'inspire and challenge children to broaden their abilities and interests in a way that goes beyond gender stereotypical choices' (2018, p. 16). England's Development Matters in the Early Years Foundation Stage (non-statutory guidance) does contain one similar sentiment, which is that adults working in ECEC settings should 'help children to learn positive attitudes and challenge negative attitudes and stereotypes, e.g. ... having a visit from a male midwife or female fire fighter' (Early Education, 2012, p. 38). However, if the EYFS were to contain a specific, stronger statement that showed a commitment to challenge traditional gender patterns and support children to make play choices regardless of gender, this may have an impact of developing the gender imbalance in two ways. Firstly, such a statement would influence the training that practitioners receive, which may promote a more gender-flexible pedagogy in settings. Secondly, such an approach may influence the career aspirations of the children attending the settings.

One setting in Sweden which takes the curriculum's direction very seriously is Egalia. This is a nursery in an affluent area of Stockholm which is taking a 'gender-neutral' approach. The practitioners don't use the pronouns 'him' and 'her' when referring to the children; instead they use the child's first name or 'hen' which is a gender-neutral pronoun (Hebbelthwaite, 2011). They aim to make sure that children's play opportunities aren't constrained by their gender and that children don't develop gendered stereotypes in their play. We know from Emilsen and Koch (2010) that men can sometimes feel like early childhood settings are a feminised environment (as the 'substitute home') and that Moss (2004) suggests that, historically, stereotypical feminine characteristics have been seen as those necessary for working with young children. It might be important to limit the extent to which children perceive the environment as 'feminised' too. Do you think that the children who attend Egalia would perceive their settings as a feminised environment?

Time to consider

Imagine you are establishing a setting in the UK that mirrors Egalia's approach. What would it look like? What would you offer? How do you think parents, practitioners and children would feel about it?

But do we need a gender-balanced workforce?

In this chapter we've focused on how to increase the number of male practitioners, yet in Chapter 6 we considered whether this was actually the best way forward, considering instead whether aiming for gender-flexible practice might be a better approach. We want to continue the discussion here which focuses on the positive outcomes of a more gender-flexible, rather than gender-balanced workforce.

Consider the quotation from Sweden's 'Curriculum for the preschool' once more. It is suggesting that the play opportunities and activities that children experience in their setting should be irrespective of their gender. The concept of gender flexibility in practitioners is similar to this; pedagogical practice should not be informed by gender. If we think back to Chapter 6, we know that there are areas of practice where men may be able to make a specific contribution – with regard to risky play, rough-and-tumble play and outdoor play. These are all important areas for children's development and therefore anyone who is training to work with young children needs to have this pedagogical understanding at the core of their training so that it becomes a gender-free pedagogy. It might make sense, also, that initiatives aimed at attracting men into the ECEC workforce would benefit from emphasising this type of play. However, it is misplaced to target these initiatives specifically at men (Emilsen and Koch, 2010) because such promotional and recruitment materials may encourage a diversity of women to apply to work with young children also.

Therefore, instead of merely looking to recruit more men into ECEC, perhaps we need to look for practitioners who can bring these apparently missing behaviours. Rather, there is a need to take the focus away from practitioner gender and turn it onto practitioner skills and dispositions. This shift in emphasis means a reduced focus on 'missing men' (Thornton and Bricheno, 2006) who can provide the 'missing pedagogy'. On the contrary, maybe we need to aim to recruit a diverse workforce with diverse skills who can be flexible and not have to rely on their personality or their gender to inform their practice. As Brownhill and Oates argued in their research into expectations of male and female practitioners (2016), it is not about the gender of the practitioner but about the professionalism and quality of pedagogy that is important. They assert that there are many 'missed opportunities … to allow professionals to be who they are' (Brownhill and Oates, 2016, p. 668). A practitioner, free of the straitjacket of expected gender behaviours (Brownhill and Oates, 2016), would also fit Warin's (2018) description of the gender-flexible practitioner. And in this way, in answer to the question posed by Nordberg (2004, cited by Brody, 2015): 'Are they mainly employed as … pre-school teachers or mainly as men?' the ECEC workforce could respond 'They are employed as professional, highly qualified and highly effective pre-school teachers'.

The suggestion that males bring something specific, or 'refreshingly different' (Wohlgemuth, 2015), to complement the female contribution can suggest that every effort needs to be made to recruit more men. At the same time, we should be encouraging female practitioners to develop these very same skills. The trouble with each of these arguments is that they both downgrade the contribution that female practitioners have made up to this point and, thus, contribute to a discourse of gender inequality.

Case study

A group of Early Childhood Studies students view TV adverts from the Swedish context which are aimed at attracting men to work with young children. They question how the men are portrayed in the adverts as the 'fun big brother' (Warin, 2015) and wonder if it is problematic to try to solve inequality issues in this way. Their tutor mentions that some countries have also taken the approach of lowering entry requirements for men.

Possible response

Some students believe that the adverts might reinforce gender stereotypes, if early years practitioners are encouraged to believe that men have a certain role to fill in the early years setting. If practitioners feel 'straitjacketed' to behave in distinct ways because of their gender, then diversity in the workforce will not be achieved.

Final reflection

If we want to increase the number of male ECEC practitioners, there are several ways that we could go about it. It is positive that both in the UK and internationally there are initiatives taking place aiming to attract men to careers in ECEC. However, many initiatives have already taken place and yet the percentage of male practitioners still remains low – standing at just 2% in the UK and at 10% in Norway, which has the greatest percentage of male practitioners. We need to consider not only the need for gender balance, but also for gender flexibility. Aiming for the 'best' practitioners, who practice a gender-neutral pedagogy may be the best way to encourage future generations of both men and women to consider a career in the ECEC workforce and also address some of the macro-level inequalities around gender that we mentioned in Chapter 1 (Introduction: Still talking about gender?).

Key points

- Currently 2% of the UK ECEC workforce is male. To increase this figure there are several initiatives taking place, including GenderEYE and MITEY, alongside those by the London Early Years Foundation and Men in Childcare.
- The issue of a lack of male practitioners has been recognised internationally. Norway has set a target of 20% male practitioners by 2020. In Sweden, the Early years curriculum promotes children to make choices that are not informed by gender stereotypes, which may increase the number of men choosing a career in ECEC in the future.
- We need to remember the concept of gender flexibility alongside gender balance. Seeking practitioners that are able to practice characteristics and qualities that are seen as both stereotypically male and female will support in having a pedagogy that is gender neutral.

Further reading

1. Warin, J. (2018) *Men in Early Childhood Education and Care: Gender Balance and Flexibility*. Great Britain: Palgrave Pilot.

   Jo Warin's book comprehensively covers the topic of men working in ECEC, based upon research she has conducted on the topic both in the UK and elsewhere, particularly Sweden.

2. Brody, D. (2014) *Men Who Teach Young Children: An International Perspective*. London: Trentham Books.

   We'd recommend having a look at this book, which examines six male practitioners in six different cultural contexts.

References

Brody, D. (2014) *Men Who Teach Young Children: An International Perspective*. London: Trentham Books.

Brody, D. (2015) 'The construction of masculine identity among men who work with young children: An international perspective', *European Early Childhood Education Research Journal*, 23(3), pp. 351–361.

Brownhill, S. and Oates, R. (2016) 'Who do you want me to be? an exploration of female and male perceptions of 'imposed' gender roles in the early years', *Education 3–13*, 45(5), pp. 658–670.

Cameron, C. (2006) 'Men in the nursery revisited: Issues of male workers and professionalism', *Contemporary Issues in Early Childhood*, 7(1), pp. 68–79.

Cushman, P. (2005) 'Let's hear it from the males: Issues facing male primary school teachers', *Teaching and Teacher Education*, 21(3), pp. 227–240.

Department for Education (2017a) *Early Years Workforce Strategy*. Available at: https://assets.publishing.service.gov.uk/government/uploads/system/uploads/attachment_data/file/596884/Workforce_strategy_02-03-2017.pdf (accessed: 18th August 2019).

Department for Education (2017b) *Statutory framework for the early years foundation stage*. Available at: www.foundationyears.org.uk/files/2017/03/EYFS_STATUTORY_FRAMEWORK_2017.pdf (accessed: 23rd August 2019).

Department for Education (2019) *Calls for More Men to Work in the Early Years*. Available at: www.gov.uk/government/news/calls-for-more-men-to-work-in-the-early-years (accessed: 18th August 2019).

Early Education (2012) *Development Matters in the Early Years Foundation Stage*. Available at: www.foundationyears.org.uk/wp-content/uploads/2012/03/Development-Matters-FINAL-PRINT-AMENDED.pdf (accessed: 18th August 2019).

Emilsen, K. and Koch, B. (2010) 'Men and women in outdoor play— changing the concepts of caring findings from Norwegian and Austrian research projects', *European Early Childhood Education Research Journal*, 18(4), pp. 543–553.

Equal Opportunities Commission (EOC) (2003) *How Can Suitable, Affordable Childcare be Provided for All Parents Who Need to Work? EOC submission to the Work and Pensions Select Committee Inquiry*, February.

European Commission (2011) *Communication from the Commission: Early Childhood Education and Care: Providing All Our Children with the Best Start for the World of Tomorrow*. Available at: https://eur-lex.europa.eu/LexUriServ/LexUriServ.do?uri=COM:2011:0066:FIN:EN:HTML (accessed: 18th August 2019).

European Commission Network on Childcare (1996) *Paper 3: Quality Targets in Services for Young Children*. Available at: www.childcarecanada.org/sites/default/files/Qualitypaperthree.pdf (accessed: 18th August 2019).

GenderEYE (2019) *GenderEYE: Our Approach*. Available at: https://gendereye.org/our-approach/(accessed: 18th August 2019).

Hebbelthwaite, C. (2011) *Sweden's 'Gender-Neutral' Pre-school*. Available at: www.bbc.co.uk/news/world-europe-14038419 (accessed: 18th August 2019).

Hedlin, M., Åberg, M. and Johansson, C. (2018) 'Fun guy and possible perpetrator: an interview study of how men are positioned within early childhood education and care', *Education Inquiry*, 10(2), pp. 95–115.

Men in The Early Years (MITEY) (2019) *The MITEY Charter*. Available at: https://miteyuk.org/sign-up-to-the-mitey-charter/(accessed: 18th August 2019).

Moss, P. (2004) 'The early childhood workforce', in: *'Developed Countries': Basic Structures and Education*. UNESCO policy brief on early childhood. Nr. 27, October 2004.

Norwegian Ministry of Children, Equality and Social Inclusion (2011) *Equality 2014 – The Norwegian Government's Gender Equality Action Plan*. Available at: www.regjeringen.no/globalassets/upload/bld/action_plan_2014.pdf (accessed: 18th August 2019).

Nursing and Midwifery Council (NMC) (2018) *The NMC Register*. Available at: www.nmc.org.uk/globalassets/sitedocuments/other-publications/the-nmc-register-2018.pdf (accessed: 18th August 2019).

Oberhuemer, P. (2011) 'The early childhood education workforce in Europe between divergencies and emergencies', *International Journal of Child Care and Education*, 5(1), pp. 55–63.

Organisation for Economic Co-operation and Development (2001) *Starting Strong*. Paris: OECD.

Organisation for Economic Co-operation and Development (2015) *The ABC of gender equality in education*. Available at: www.oecd.org/pisa/keyfindings/pisa-2012-results-gender-eng.pdf (accessed: 18th August 2019).

Peeters, J., Rohrmann, T. and Emilsen, K. (2015) 'Gender balance in ECEC: why is there so little progress?', *European Early Childhood Education Research Journal*, 23(3), pp. 302–314.

Perkins, H., Edwards, T. and O'Sullivan, J. (2019) *Men in Childcare: Does It Matter to Children, What Do they Say? (Stage 2)*. Available at: www.leyf.org.uk/wp-content/uploads/2019/02/Men-in-Childcare-stage-2-Final-v7-JO-HP-TE-compressed.pdf (accessed: 18th August 2019).

Rolfe, H. (2005) Men in childcare. *National Institute of Economic and Social Research*. Available at: www.koordination-maennerinkitas.de/uploads/media/Rolfe-Heather.pdf (accessed: 18th August 2019).

Rolfe, H. (2006) 'Where are the men? gender segregation in the childcare and early years sector', *National Institute Economic Review*, 195(1), pp. 103–117.

The Royal Ministry of Children, Equality and Social Inclusion (2015) *Gender equality in practice: equal opportunities for women and men*. Available at: www.regjeringen.no/contentassets/cb13bb1a651942b9ae61d329e85c2c7e/gender-equality-in-practice—white-paper.pdf (accessed: 18th August 2019).

Scottish Government (2018a) *Men Employed in Childcare: FOI Release*. Available at: www.gov.scot/publications/foi-18-00823/(accessed: 18th August 2019).

Scottish Government (2018b) *Encouraging More Men into Childcare*. Available at: www.gov.scot/news/encouraging-more-men-into-childcare/(accessed: 18th August 2019).

Statistics Norway (2018) *Women and Men in Norway*. Available at: www.ssb.no/en/befolkning/artikler-og-publikasjoner/_attachment/347081?_ts=1632b8bcba0 (accessed: 18th August 2019).

Statistics Norway (2019) *Employees in Kindergartens and Schools*. Available at: www.ssb.no/en/utdanning/statistikker/utdansatte (accessed: 18th August 2019).

Sumsion, J. (2000) 'Negotiating otherness: A male early childhood educator's gender positioning', *International Journal of Early Years Education*, 8(2), pp. 129–140. doi: 10.1080/09669760050046174.

Swedish Institute (2019) *Preschool – A Place to Grow*. Available at: https://sweden.se/society/play-is-key-in-preschool/(accessed: 18th August 2019).

Swedish National Agency for Education (2018) *Curriculum for the Preschool*. Available at: www.sweducare.se/Portals/Sweducare/Users/229/57/3557/The%20Swedish%20 curriculum%20for%20preschool%20lpfo%CC%8818.pdf?ver=2019-05-20-094109-510 (accessed: 18th August 2019).

TheyWorkForYou (2019) *Early Years – in the Scottish Parliament on 6th March 2019*. Available at: www.theyworkforyou.com/sp/?id=2019-03-06.21.0 (accessed: 18th August 2019).

Thornton, M. and Bricheno, P. (2006) *Missing Men in Education*. Stoke on Trent: Trentham Books.

Wane, K. (2019) *The Expansion of Early Learning and Childcare*. Available at: https://digitalpublications.parliament.scot/ResearchBriefings/Report/2019/4/16/The-expansion-of-early-learning-and-childcare (accessed: 18th August 2019).

Warin, J. (2015) 'Pioneers, professionals, playmates, protectors, 'poofs' and 'paedos': Swedish male pre-school teachers' construction of their identities', in: S. Brownhill, J. Warin, and I. Wernersson (eds) *Men, Masculinities and Teaching in Early Childhood Education: International Perspectives on Gender and Care*. Oxon: Routledge.

Warin, J. (2017) 'Conceptualising the value of male practitioners in early childhood education and care: gender balance or gender flexibility', *Gender and Education*, 31(3), pp. 293–308. doi: 10.1080/09540253.2017.1380172.

Warin, J. (2018) *Men in Early Childhood Education and Care: Gender Balance and Flexibility*. Great Britain: Palgrave Pilot.

Williams, R. (2017) 'Why are there so few male nurses?', *The Guardian*, 1 March. Available at: https://www.theguardian.com/healthcare-network/2017/mar/01/why-so-few-male-nurses (accessed: 20th November 2019).

Wohlgemuth, G. (2015) 'Why do men choose to become social educators? A profession continuously in pursuit of male colleagues', *European Early Childhood Education Research Journal*, 23(3), pp. 392–404.

PART

A gendered society

CHAPTER

8

Is caring gendered?

Introduction

Care is such a simple word, isn't it? It's a word we use in our everyday conversations probably without reflecting on what it really means; the subtitle of the Statutory framework for the EYFS (Department for Education, 2017) is 'Setting the standards for learning, development and *care* for children from birth to five' (our emphasis) so it is obviously an important consideration when we think about young children; that's why we have devoted a whole chapter to discussing it here. In Part I of this book we looked at the gendered child; Part II took us to the gendered early years setting, and we have now arrived at Part III where our attention turns to a more macro level where we will look at three gendered issues in society. The first, in this chapter, is the idea of care. One thing that is noteworthy is the idea that, when we are thinking about caring for children, we can often assume this is something women do best. Certainly, we hear the argument a lot that caring, in terms of nurturing, may be something that women do naturally; 'that's because women can carry babies' is often how the argument goes, without making the connection that not all women can, or indeed want to, carry babies. Those who put this argument forward will often stress that they are not asserting that men don't care about children, it's just that it is not a natural disposition for them. This is a very problematic argument, or we could call it another script, and it is one we are going to explore and examine in this chapter. In the previous part we looked at the nature of the early years workforce and explored some of the reasons it is seen as a female profession. This chapter will build on this discussion by considering the concept of 'caring' and why it may be seen as a female disposition. We will:

- develop your understanding of the notion of 'caring',
- explore and critique some of the reasons why 'caring' continues to be regarded as a female skill and disposition,
- highlight some of the perceived differences in how males and females demonstrate 'caring' behaviours and practice.

The chapter will explore the gendered nature of caring and discuss how caring as an attribute can be linked to biological or social forces. We will look at whether gendered differences in caring exist, or whether there is simply a perception that this is the case (Noddings, 1984). We will also explore what the implications for young children are if they perceive caring to be a female attribute.

How can we define caring?

Theories of caring

We know that we can link children's ability to care to their moral development but what about adults? How can we better examine their caring behaviours? Just as with children we can look at theories of moral development, so too with adults we can draw on theoretical models to help us understand a bit more about care. In this part of the chapter we will draw on some of these key theorists, such as Gilligan (1982) and Noddings (1984).

Gilligan's work (1982) was important because it turned previous understanding of moral development on its head. Up to this point what we knew was informed by white male psychologists often working with male children. Gilligan highlighted this fact; she had been a student of one of the most seminal theorists in moral development (Kohlberg, 1966) and the way that it had led to women, who may have been socialised to emphasise 'relationships and care over logic and justice' (Gilligan and Goldberg, 2000, p. 702) and being thought of as 'morally inferior' (ibid). Gilligan believed that the caring dispositions of women and the 'traditional positioning of femininity in service of the other' (McLeod, 2006, p. 230) was closely associated with the mother/child relationship in the earliest years of a child's life. McLeod (2006, p. 290) draws on Gilligan's work (1977, 1982) to describe how:

> While both boys and girls initially identify with the mother, the process of individuation is different. Girls can remain identified with the mother, a relationship that predisposes them to certain emotional traits such as concern and empathy for others and interdependence. Boys, in contrast, need to separate from the mother, and this predisposes them to autonomy, detachment and objectivity.
>
> (Gilligan, 1977, 1982).

Nell Noddings drew on her work when she describes the close link between women's moral development and the idea of caring:

> Women, perhaps the majority of women, prefer to discuss moral problems in terms of concrete situations. They approach moral problems not as intellectual problems to be solved by abstract reasoning but as concrete problems to be lived and to be solved in living. Their approach is founded in caring
>
> (Noddings, 1984, p. 96)

Nodding's seminal work, *Caring: A Feminine Approach to Ethics and Moral Education* first published in 1984 considered the place of relationships in care theory. She emphasised that the 'one-caring' is as dependent on the 'cared-for' as vice versa making a 'distinct contribution to the relation and establishes it as caring' (Noddings, 1984, p. xiii).

Early years practitioners, in some respects, have much in common with the profession of nursing, particularly when we consider the concept of emotional labour (Gray, 2010). In Gray's study all of the nurses interviewed believed this was a key part of their work and described it as making the patient feel 'safe, comfortable and at home' (2010, p. 351). We could easily substitute the word 'patient' for 'child' and imagine the key person in an early years setting having the same sense of responsibility towards their young charges. Both professions are perceived to have an element of caring and, as such, are seen as gendered professions. The difference is there has been more success, up to this point, in addressing the gender balance in nursing that there has been in early years practice. Gray (2010) describes how nursing has struggled to shake off its Florence Nightingale image of 'angel, mother and natural carer' (p. 350) and in many ways the early years practitioner is seen in this way too – as one who is just doing what comes naturally, acting as a 'mother substitute' *in loco parentis*. Care then becomes to be seen as something you can just do because of your gender.

Theories of caring are directly related to feminist thinking and what it is to be a woman. Key writers in this area, such as Gilligan (1982) and Noddings (1984), have helped both elevate the concept of caring from a low status activity and also enabled us to understand how it has evolved as such a gendered notion.

Caring for or caring about

We could argue that it is not the word 'care' that is problematic but rather it is the preposition that follows it; we can decide, for example, to follow it with the word 'for'. Many may see the role of the primary school teacher, not as one who should 'care for' children, that surely this is a phrase that relates to the emotional bond that parents share with children. They would argue that such a phrase diminishes the role of the primary school teacher and reduces its sense of professionalism. Thornton and Bricheno (2006) certainly argue that the role of the teacher, however much legally they are supposed to be *in loco parentis*, is not to be a substitute mummy or daddy. They are talking about the context of the primary school teacher and whether young children need 'father figures' in the classroom (look back at our discussion in Chapter 6 (What is the impact of the gender imbalance in the early years workforce?)); we might suggest that there is a different requirement in the early years setting, with much younger children who are developing secondary attachments so important for their well-being. Still, it must be highlighted that a key issue of the debates around the status of those who work with young children centres on whether they are 'caring for' or 'caring about'.

'Caring about' is a very different concept to 'caring for'. It can still contain elements of professional passion and affective response, but it seems to be viewed as a more professional, higher-status form of caring. The primary school teacher can care about outcomes for the children in her/his care without necessarily feeling they have to be nurturing towards those children; the early years practitioner can harness the 'passion' (Moyles, 2001) or 'emotional labour' (Colley, 2006) for their work to really impact positively on children's development without necessarily feeling that they have to play the 'mummy' or 'daddy' role in the workplace. However, for some, both in and outside the workforce there can be a tension between these two types of caring.

The difficulties arise when these two kinds of caring are confused and there is an expectation on the practitioner that they can and should relate to a child as a parent relates to a child. This is problematic in many ways and marginalises those who have an excellent understanding of pedagogy and child development but little interest in adopting a 'mumsy' role. It also can contribute to the low number of men attracted to the workforce that we talk about in Chapter 5 (Why is there a gender imbalance in the early years workforce?). Thornton and Bricheno (2006) draw on Ashley and Lee's work (2003) on attachment to explain the clear distinction that should be made:

> Ashley and Lee (2003) use attachment theory to differentiate parental "caring for" children from the teacher's role of "caring about" the children they teach and to underpin their argument that all children need and want good carers and good teachers, irrespective of their gender. Teachers are not carers in a familial Bowlbian sense. They are educators with a duty of care for their pupils, which is different. It is not a permanent relationship. They cannot fulfil the attachment role, though they may be important significant others in a child's development, through "caring about" their well-being and education. The teacher's role is distinct from that of the home or primary carer, and is concerned with widening independence and enhancing experience beyond a secure and reliable family environment.
>
> (Thornton and Bricheno, 2006, p. 8)

Therefore, to sum up this section of the chapter, we can see that when considering how the term 'care' should be defined in the context of working with young children we need to consider the preposition that follows it; are we talking about caring *for* a child, as in professional love, or are we talking about caring *about* a child's learning and development, as in our professionality? Many practitioners would answer it is both of these types of care; however, this viewpoint can be problematic in two distinct ways. Firstly, it might discourage those who may not see themselves as particularly nurturing from a career in working with young children. Secondly, the fact that looking after young children is seen as caring for them, when caring continues to be seen as a low-value activity, helps to continue the discourse that working with young children requires little skill.

The passion of the early years practitioner

Practitioners will define passion in different ways depending on the context they are working within but certainly it is a word that practitioners often use (Moyles, 2001) or, some might say, overuse, to describe how they engage with their work. But what do they actually mean when they use the word 'passion'? Do practitioners have a shared understanding of this term? Colley (2006) uses the phrase 'emotional labour' to describe the passion and commitment to their vocation that practitioners can adopt but warns at the same time that this disposition is one that can be taken advantage of. Moyles (2001) holds a similar view suggesting that this passion 'can work for or against them' (p. 81). However, she also demonstrates how this passion can be harnessed both for the good of children and the workforce in general by providing opportunities for practitioners to work with researchers and engage in critical reflection on this element of their role.

However rewarding it may be working with young children and their families, this is not a job for the faint-hearted. There are many reasons that people want to work with young children (Cooke and Lawton, 2008). Many will want to have a positive impact on outcomes for young children's lives; for example, Koch and Farquhar (2015) cite Williams' assertion (2011) that they have 'a desire to be involved in something socially significant' (p. 381). Yet at the same time they are not rewarded financially for this important work and their voices 'are rarely heard' (Brownhill and Oates, 2016, p. 658). Another key idea used in tandem with this concept of professional passion is the term 'professional love'; we will consider this in the next section of the chapter.

Professional love

Mothers of young babies are encouraged to return to employment by government policy but what factors are important to them when they look for childcare for these very youngest children? For example, are they looking for a temporary replacement for themselves – someone who will impact most positively on their child's development – or a combination of both these aspects, e.g. an 'educarer'? Page (2011), while exploring mothers' perceptions of 'professional love' shown towards their babies, cites the work of Uttal (1996) to define the types of care sought:

> Custodial care: mothers … saw themselves as their child's main carer and it was they who set the boundaries of how their child spent their time with the carer

> Surrogate care: mothers … saw themselves as the primary carer but recognized the emotional and physical input from the carer, similar to their role as mother.
>
> Co-ordinated care: women who did not consider their role as mother replaced but instead recognized the role of the carer as important and complementary to their mother role.
>
> (Page, 2011, p. 311)

It is noteworthy how it is both the (female) mother and the female carer who are highlighted in this kind of research; the father's voice appears silent as if care is only something for the female to deal with.

In a further article, Page (2013) argues that the female's ability to be a good mother is judged not only by her own interactions with her children but also by how she chooses who is going to take her place when she goes back to work and whether this involves a seeking out of professional love to replace her own when she is not there. We would be justified in arguing that this does not happen to the 'good father'. These working mothers have already slipped down the hierarchy of good mothers by returning to work at all; those at the top are the white, middle-class mothers who, according to Dalli (1999) – cited in Page (2013) – are the 'good mothers [who] want to look after their child at all times' (2013, p. 548). Of course, Dalli was writing two decades ago and there will be other factors, such as cultural beliefs, which inform whether a parent can employ others to professionally 'love' their child.

Both the geographical and the cultural context could contribute to whether the practitioner is allowed to show 'love' towards their children and indeed if this is a required part of their job specification. For example, Campbell-Barr et al. (2015) carried out an interesting comparative study to consider how practitioners in both the English and the Hungarian contexts believed the notion of love was important in their interactions with young children. They found that the Hungarian practitioners had much more freedom to show love towards the children in their settings whereas the English practitioners were constrained due to 'managerialist and entrepreneurial discourses … creating tensions with more emotional dispositions of being caring, supportive, and empathic' (p. 311). It is suggested then that the notion of love has much higher status within the context of the early years workforce in the Hungarian context than it has in the English context.

Some parents, usually referred to in the research literature as 'mothers', want the person who is looking after their child to show love towards them. This could be because they are concerned about their own status as a 'good mother' in the eyes of society. We have argued, however, that this could be dependent on the type of society they belong to.

Let's conclude this section of the chapter by recalling that caring can be defined in many ways but caring appears to be a professed necessary skill for those who work with young children. Whether this type of care is the same as the care that a parent shows to a child is open to discussion and perhaps we need two different words to differentiate between these two different kinds of relationships. The same is true with the concept of love; it may seem strange to use this term in the context of professional relationships, but some research literature suggests that in fact professional love is a key idea in the realm of caring professions.

Time to consider

How do you feel about the role of the early years practitioner and the concept of professional love? Try to come up with a definition of professional love by thinking about the behaviours (practices), dispositions and skills it could be comprised of. You may like to use Table 8.1 to help you.

How is having a caring disposition linked to gender?

The link between caring and personality

To help us answer the question above, we can first turn to the discipline of psychology to ask whether having a caring personality is something inherent that you are born with or something that develops because of socialisation. However, as always with psychology, the answer is 'it depends'. Some theorists, like Eysenck, suggested that personality is biological and linked to an over or underactive nervous system. As such, it was possible to test personality in an experimental way. For example, there is the lemon drop test – if given a lemon drop, introverts would produce more saliva than extroverts because of their overactive nervous system. Eysenck also thought that, for example, you could test for an inherent criminal tendency, suggesting extroverts were harder to condition and therefore more likely to be criminal. So, in theory, if Eysenck was correct, having a caring personality would be biologically determined and you could study the corresponding nervous system reaction from birth.

TABLE 8.1 Defining professional love

Behaviours/Practices	Skills	Dispositions

However, other people, like Freud, believed that personality is not inherent but rather is shaped by experience from a very young age. So, for example, children who have a conflict during breastfeeding or weaning can become orally fixated, which will impact on the development of personality traits emerging from around one or two years old. At a later stage, say three years onwards, they will then develop different traits depending on their reaction to potty training. So, for Freud, a child's personality, and therefore the caring disposition, is formed between birth and puberty, becoming more and more apparent in the child's behaviour as they grow.

Then, of course, there are the behaviourists who would suggest that personality is both learned and in theory could be relearned. However, the personality theory that dominates at present, and which some suggest is supported by the best empirical evidence, is the 'big five' types of personality. These five types are:

1 Openness to experience,
2 Conscientiousness,
3 Agreeableness,
4 Extraversion–introversion,
5 Neuroticism–stability.

The last two have a biological basis, whereas the first three are more products of upbringing, but all are maturational to some extent. The challenge with personality testing is that most tests involve self-reporting such as the Eysenck Personality Questionnaire (EPQ) or the Hogan Personality inventory; furthermore, they are mostly designed for adults. Of course, self-reporting is not an ideal way to measure whether someone has a caring personality; it is more a measure of whether an individual 'thinks' they have a caring personality. For example, if females have been socialised to believe they should be caring, they may self-report this aspect of their personality. Even more difficult would be to measure the development of a caring personality in children, particularly if based on the reports of their parents.

Some evidence, then, would have us believe that caring is a disposition predominantly displayed by the female and that this is because of innate, biological forces. This argument is supported by the 'common-sense' notion that because it is the female of the species that gives birth and breastfeeds them naturally, they have a kind of 'caring' gene. Other evidence, from the discipline of psychology, uses personality research to suggest that the female is more likely to display personality traits which align with nurturing and caring.

The link between caring and social forces

To consider the link between caring and social forces we need to think about how girls are taught to care and at the same time whether boys are also taught *not* to care. In addition, we must also be aware of the dynamic nature both of childhood and of gender to consider whether this socialisation has changed in recent times as more traditional gender norms have been challenged and disrupted.

We only have to look at toys marketed at girls to see the emphasis on care. This could be caring about babies (dolls) and animals (unicorns), caring about the home (cleaning and cooking equipment) or caring about what they look like (make-up, beauty and jewellery-type toys). James (2019, p. 2) writes:

> in order to best understand the established gender "norms" in a society, it is pertinent to observe the behaviours of others surrounding one another. Norms within a society are the usual, typical or standard behaviours that are placed on individuals before they are even born.

We can add that, once they are born, adults will reinforce these norms through the selection of gender-specific toys, or environments, they give them. For example, MacPhee and Prendergast's research (2018), which audited the content of children's bedrooms, discovered how items found in this context can set up gendered norms.

So, what might MacPhee and Prendergast have found in boys' bedrooms? How are boys targeted with certain toy choices? Think of little boys you know – do they have guns (to kill), tools (to fix), sports-related and car-related toys? James (2019) believes that boys are drawn to certain toys, and discouraged from playing with others, by the packaging used; this is not necessarily to do with colour but rather pictures of children playing with them. Can you imagine, for example, packaging for a doll which included pictures of a boy playing with it? Why this should be so problematic in the 21st century is difficult to fathom when many dads take full responsibility for childcare. James, too, is writing in the context of 2019; this could suggest, then, that although some manufacturers and shops have tried to adopt a more unisex approach, gender norms are still entrenched and it is very difficult to genuinely disrupt the scripts which focus on what boys and girls should play with.

Anecdotally, we would suggest that parents seem to be quite happy to let children make their own toy choices in 2019 and may even actively encourage boys to play with dolls or toy cooking equipment. Certainly, in an early years setting, practitioners would be very aware of not gender labelling toys and thereby encouraging children to play with a full range. However, in encouraging children to join in nursery rhymes and songs, really important activities in terms of young children's early literacy skills, both parents and practitioners could inadvertently be passing on gendered messages about who does the caring. Kumar (2019, p. 301) writes:

> Since childhood, gender stereotypes have been implanted into our minds through nursery rhymes. Men and women are conditioned to behave

in a particular manner based on the societal norms which are predominantly patriarchal. Through this, children tend to internalise these behavioural patterns which they pass on to the future generations. While boys are seen playing in the ground and are depicted as the earning and the responsible member of the family, girls are often seen playing with dolls, doing household chores, gardening, etc. Hence, the stereotypes imposed on children restrict their identity. This leads to gradual internalisation of these norms thereby conditioning children to perform these constructed gender roles.

This is a difficult one and some practitioners may change some of the words to avoid reinforcing such stereotypes; however, it does help us to realise how ingrained ideas about gender can be in our culture and how we are continually passing these ideas on to children, however inadvertently.

Historically, the way children have been socialised throughout the centuries means that girls have been indoctrinated almost from birth to believe that they are the natural carers. At the same time, boys have been led to believe that this is not a natural, or at times appropriate, thing for them to do. As discussions around gender have developed, it has become more acceptable for men to demonstrate caring behaviours by, for example, moving into traditionally female professions such as nursing or Early Years; however, entrenched attitudes take a long time to shift. Conversely, is it, or will it ever be acceptable for a female to admit that she does not have a caring disposition?

Time to consider

Think about nursery rhymes and traditional songs that you learned as a young child and that perhaps you use with children now. What gendered messages could they be passing on to young children? For example, what about the following favourite?

> Miss Polly had a dolly who was sick, sick, sick
>
> So, she phoned for the doctor to be quick, quick, quick
>
> The doctor came with his hat and his bag
>
> And he knocked at the door with a rat-a-tat-tat.
>
> He looked at the dolly and he shook his head
>
> And he said "Miss Polly, put her straight to bed!"
>
> He wrote on the paper for a pill, pill, pill,
>
> "I'll be back in the morning with my bill, bill, bill!"

What are the implications for young children if they perceive caring to be a female attribute?

We would argue then that it does matter that children can attend an early years setting and perceive the norm to be that the practitioners will be predominantly female. In this way the idea that 'caring' is something that the female does will be reinforced, encouraging children to continue thinking in binary ways about the different things that men and women do. They will take this thinking with them through childhood and into adulthood if nobody bothers to disrupt the notion. Therefore, the potential of some individuals will remain locked up if they feel that their behaviours and practices have to be constrained to gender-specific ones.

There are many reasons why caring has come to be perceived as a female disposition and skill. Firstly, there is a narrative which focuses on the female disposition to care; that their ability to care is biological and innate. Secondly, socialisation has contributed to the continual reinforcement of woman as carer, while minimising the role of the male in this interaction. Thirdly, and a key part of this socialisation, is the very fact that young children are predominantly surrounded by women 'looking after' them in the early years setting. This situation can continue to reinforce the message that women + caring = the norm.

Time to consider

Think about all the people who have cared for you in your life. Think about their gender and also whether you feel they cared for you in different ways because of this. Does this link at all to the different ways that males and females are said to care?

Case study

Nicos has just started working as an early years practitioner in a baby room. In his induction, he was told that he will not be responsible for nappy-changing duties, as previously parents have requested that male practitioners are not involved in this. There are many things to consider in these two short sentences; here are some questions to help you:

- Should Nicos, as a male practitioner, be in the baby room?
- If it is considered appropriate that he is there, should he be constrained in his duties?
- Why do you think parents have really made this request?

A gendered society

- Why has the setting management team made this rule?
- Who holds the power in this situation? Does it matter?
- What do you think the appropriate course of action should be and why?

Possible response

If we say a professional, regardless of their gender, has the essentials skills to work in a baby room, then we should not be saying they cannot perform certain aspects of their role. Either they need additional training, or they need to be working at a higher grade, but not because of their gender! Imagine if a setting said female practitioners were not allowed to use the outside environment because of something a parent may have read. Parents who have made the nappy-changing request may have been impacted by a very problematic discourse which equates the male early years practitioner with paedophilia – the management team need to urgently disrupt this discourse.

Final reflection

To conclude this chapter, let us remind ourselves that 'care' has proved to be a slippery term which is difficult to define. Yet at the same time it is a heavily gendered concept. Regardless of the great strides forwards women have made in the last two decades, along with some movement of men into what were thought to be traditionally female professions, employment which contains a caring element is still considered to be more appropriate for women and is therefore seen to be lower status. When literature does examine men's caring behaviours, it can categorise them as different to women's and, at times, suggests that men are privileged in being able to choose the caring they want to do, because of structural patriarchy, as opposed to women, who end up having to do all the caring that men have selected not to do.

Key points

- Care and caring are not neutral concepts; we need to examine closely how our definitions of them have come about.
- When we think of care and the caring professions, we immediately think of women having the appropriate skills and dispositions to carry them out.
- Developmental psychology and socialisation theories can help us understand gender differences in caring behaviours.

Further reading

1. Campbell-Barr, V., Georgeson, J. and Nagy Varga, A.N. (2015) 'Developing professional early childhood educators in England and Hungary: Where has all the love gone?', *European Education*, 47(4), 311–330.

    This is a really interesting journal article which we referred to in this chapter. It examines attitudes towards professional love both in the English and the Hungarian context.

2. Kumar, S.S. (2019) 'Nursery rhymes: A medium to internalise gender stereotypes', *International Journal of English Language, Literature in Humanities*, 7(6)

    Did you find the discussion on nursery rhymes fascinating? We certainly did! Have a look at Kumar's article which influenced this part of our discussion.

References

Ashley, M. and Lee, J. (2003) *Women Teaching Boys*. Stoke-on-Trent: Trentham books.

Brooker, L. (2015) 'Cultural capital in the preschool years: Can the state 'compensate' for the family?' in: L. Alanen, E. Brooker and B. Mayall (eds) *Childhood with Bourdieu*. Hampshire: Palgrave MacMillan.

Brownhill, S. and Oates, R. (2016). Who do you want me to be? An exploration of female and male perceptions of 'imposed' gender roles in the early years, *Education 3–13*, 45(5), pp. 658–670.

Campbell-Barr, V., Georgeson, J. and Nagy Varga, A.N. (2015) 'Developing professional early childhood educators in England and Hungary: Where has all the love gone?' *European Education*, 47(4), pp. 311–330.

Colley, H. (2006) 'Learning to labour with feeling: Class, gender and emotion in childcare education and training', *Contemporary Issues in Early Childhood*, 7(1), pp. 15–29.

Cooke, C. and Lawton, K. (2008) *For Love or Money: Pay, Progression and Professionalization in the 'Early Years' Workforce*. London: Institute for Public Policy Research.

Dalli, C. (1999) 'Learning to be in childcare: Mothers' stories of their child's 'Settling-In'', *European Early Childhood Education Research Journal*, 7(2), pp. 53–66.

Department for Education (2017) *Statutory Framework for the Early Years Foundation Stage*. Available at: www.foundationyears.org.uk/files/2017/03/EYFS_STATUTORY_FRAMEWORK_2017.pdf (accessed: 19th August 2019).

Gilligan, C. (1977) In a different voice: Women's conception of self and morality, *Harvard Education Review*, 47(4), pp. 481–517.

Gilligan, C. (1982) *In a Different Voice*. Boston, MA: Harvard University Press.

Gilligan, C. and Goldberg, M.F. (2000) 'An interview with Carol Gilligan: restoring lost voices', *The Phi Delta Kappan*, 81(9), pp. 701–704.

Gray, B. (2010) 'Emotional labour, gender and professional stereotypes of emotional and physical contact, and personal perspectives on the emotional labour of nursing', *Journal of Gender Studies*, 19(4), pp. 349–360.

James, L. (2019) 'Gendering toys: How pink and blue define life outcomes for children', *Writing Across the Curriculum*. 38. Available at: https://digitalcommons.sacredheart.edu/wac_prize/38/ (accessed: 27th August 2019).

Koch, B. and Farquhar, S. (2015) 'Breaking through the glass doors: Men working in early childhood education and care with particular reference to research and experience in Austria and New Zealand', *European Early Childhood Education Research Journal*, 23(3), pp. 380–391.

Kohlberg, L. (1966) 'A cognitive-developmental analysis of children's sex-role concepts and attitudes', in: E. Maccoby (ed.) *The Development Of Sex Differences*. London: Tavistock.

Kumar, S.S. (2019) 'Nursery rhymes: A medium to internalise gender stereotypes', *International Journal of English Language, Literature in Humanities*, 7(6), pp. 301–308.

MacPhee, D. and Prendergast, S. (2018) 'Room for improvement: Girls' and boys' home environments are still gendered', *Sex Roles*, 80(5–6), pp. 332–346.

McLeod, J. (2006) 'Working out intimacy', in: M. Arnot and M.M. An Ghaill (eds) *The RoutledgeFalmer reader in Gender and Education*. Abingdon: Routledge..

Moyles, J. (2001) 'Passion, paradox and professionalism in early years education', *Early Years*, 21(2), pp. 81–95.

Noddings, N. (1984) *Caring, a Feminine Approach to Ethics & Moral Education*. London: University of California Press.

Page, J. (2011) 'Do mothers want professional carers to love their babies?' *Journal of Early Childhood Research*, 9(3), pp. 310–323.

Page, J. (2013) 'Will the 'good' [working] mother please stand up? Professional and maternal concerns about education, care and love', *Gender and Education*, 25(5), pp. 548–563.

Thornton, M. and Bricheno, P. (2006). *Missing Men in Education*. Stoke on Trent: Trentham Books.

Uttal, L. (1996) 'Custodial care, surrogate care, and coordinated care: Employed mothers and the meaning of child care', *Gender and Society*, 10(3), pp. 291–311.

CHAPTER

9

Motherhood and fatherhood

Do parents engage with their children in gendered ways?

Introduction

In the previous chapter we looked at the concept of care and how it is often seen as a female attribute. We suggested that an argument often used, although – we hastened to reaffirm – not one we subscribe to, is that women are natural nurturers because they carry children and can become mothers who nurture through breastfeeding. Let us continue this discussion by thinking about what we understand about the concepts of motherhood and fatherhood. We want you to take the verbs 'to father' and 'to mother' and to think of when you have heard a sentence in which each are used. For example, if we think of the phrase 'to father', we may come up with the sentence 'he fathered a child'. 'To father' is seen here as a synonym of 'to procreate' – a one-off undertaking, a completed action. Now what about a sentence you have heard that contains the verb 'to mother'. For us what comes to mind is when we hear people say in a disapproving way that a woman is 'mothering someone', i.e. being overbearing and overprotective towards them. In contrast to the single action of 'to father', 'to mother' is seen as a continuous process – an ongoing act of care.

Now we recognise that this is a simplified argument; if we look elsewhere for definitions we see that the *OED* defines 'to father' as 'to act as a father to; to look after' as one of its secondary definitions. This is similar (although there are differences) to one of the *OED* definitions of 'to mother', which is 'to bring up, take care of, or protect as a mother; to look after in a (sometimes excessively) kindly and protective way'. We are not trying to suggest that fathering is a one-off act or that mothers are superior in terms of how they care and protect their children. But what we are trying to demonstrate is that, through an introductory look at how these words are used in everyday language, we can see that there might be tensions in how the concepts of 'fathering' and 'mothering' are perceived. How would you define 'to father' and 'to mother'? Your definitions might include the notion of being a parent. This creates a new challenge: how would you define the verb 'to parent'? The *OED*'s definition is 'to be or act as a parent'. But which? Mother or father? And does it matter – do male and female parents behave differently, anyway? If they do, what might be the impact of this? Those are the types of questions we are going to explore in this chapter as we:

- build your understanding of some perceived gendered differences in how parents engage with their children,
- explore some of the ways it is suggested that these differences impact on a child's development,
- highlight the tensions that exist when we discuss the concepts of 'Fathering' and 'mothering'

This chapter will explore the special role that fathers and mothers are perceived to have in the lives of their children and whether they might impact on their development in specific ways; it will also ask if there is sufficient evidence to suggest gendered differences in parenting style (Clarke, 2009; Fagan et al., 2014; Lamb, 2010; Winsler et al., 2005). We will also recognise the tension between the two competing perspectives that, on the one hand, fathers can often be sidelined (Fatherhood Institute, 2013) and, on the other hand, single mothers or their children should not be seen in a deficit way (Golombok, 2016).

Do mothers and fathers engage with their children in different ways?

Let us start by going back to those definitions of 'to mother' and 'to father'. Do the differing definitions suggest that mothers and fathers will engage with their children in different ways? And is this the case in your personal or professional experiences? Do you have evidence to back up your thoughts? If you talk to a peer or colleague you might find that you do not agree about whether there are differences in how mothers and fathers behave. This is true of researchers too; research literature on parenting does not always agree on whether there are gendered parental differences. In this section we are going to look at what the literature says about how mothers and fathers engage with their children in three domains – discipline, language and play.

Discipline

Do you think mothers and fathers discipline, interact and behave with their children in different ways? Many people think 'yes' (including parents themselves – more on that later), yet a lot of the research literature says 'no'. Lamb (2010, p. 10), having reviewed the literature in this field, suggests that it is not gender-related characteristics that play a role in how parents behave with their children, but rather their own parental characteristics. He suggests that 'students of socialization have consistently found that parental warmth, nurturance, and closeness are associated with positive child outcomes regardless of whether the parent involved is a mother or a father' (ibid.). In other words, it is not the gender of the parents that is significant, but rather how the parent is interacting with their child. In addition, Lamb (ibid.) asserts that 'the description of mothering largely resemble[s] the description of fathering'. This is echoed by Fagan et al. (2014), when they claim that 'there is not enough evidence to conclude that the constructs of fathering and mothering are unique' (p. 390).

Yet it has been found that parents themselves sometimes believe that mothers and fathers engage with their children in different ways. A study by Winsler et al. (2005) found that mothers and fathers identified differences in their parenting styles. They investigated how parents in the same home self-reported their own parenting style and also that of their partners. They discovered that fathers generally 'perceive their spouses to be more authoritative, more permissive, and less authoritarian than themselves, whereas mothers only perceive themselves to be more authoritative than fathers' (2005, p. 1). When mothers and fathers had a similar parenting style, they were more accurate in reporting their partner's parenting style than when their styles differed. Winsler et al. (2005, p. 9) argue that their findings suggest 'parenting style and perceptions of parenting style may vary as a function of parental gender'.

We do need to consider at this point why it might be believed that men and women parent differently, when evidence suggests this is not the case. Remember back in Chapter 5 (Why is there a gender imbalance in the early years workforce?) we spoke about the idea of discourses and scripts – those stories that are told about something which may influence and reinforce stereotypes? Lamb (2010, p. 272) talks about how 'the narrative [about parents] is stereotypically gendered and depicts men, compared to women, as less caring and more abusive toward children in general'. Yet while stereotypical views of men may be that they are less sensitive or caring than women, a report by Clarke (2009) states that men are seen as being just as sensitive and caring as their female counterparts. If this surprises you then it is worth examining your own assumptions here about whether you perceive there to be differences between mother' and fathers' behaviour with their children.

Language

Another way that there may be differences in how mothers and fathers engage with their children is in relation to the language they use with them. Several studies suggest that mothers and fathers use language with children in diverse ways (Clarke, 2009; Pancsofar and Vernon-Feagans, 2006; Raeburn, 2014; Yogman and Garfield, 2016). For example, Pancsofar and Vernon-Feagans (2006) conducted a study where they videoed 24-month-old children playing with their mothers and fathers. Then, when the children reached 36 months old they completed a language test. Upon analysing the observations of the families playing, they found that mothers spoke more than the fathers, yet on further analysis 'mothers and fathers differed on the quantity of output but not on the quality of their output' (2006, p. 582), for instance because there was not a difference in how many questions each asked. When the children's language tests were compared with data from the observations, the researchers found that there was no link between the mothers' language input at 24 months and children's language development at 36 months. However, there was a link between the fathers' language input in the observations at 24 months and the children's performance in the language test at 36 months once other variables like childcare and parental education were considered.

Raeburn (2014) has also found differences in the language input that mothers and fathers provide. He discusses how mothers will ensure that their language fits with what the child already knows whereas fathers will challenge by introducing unknown terminology. If this is indeed the case then there is an alignment with the traditional idea of female as carer (Clarke, 2009; Lamb, 2000, 2010), finely attuned to the child, and male as provider (Marshall et al., 2014) providing more language and more experiences. If you think back to Chapter 6 (What is the impact of the gender imbalance in the early years workforce?), this fits with what we said about male caregivers being able to offer a specific contribution to practice through risky play, because men encourage children to take more risks and challenges (LEYF, 2012).

Play

Some studies reveal how fathers play in different ways to mothers. Clarke (2009) and Lamb (2000; 2010) both reveal a 'play versus caregiving' dichotomy, with mothers choosing the 'caregiver role' and fathers the 'player' role. It is also suggested that when choosing to play, mothers will be drawn more to using objects and resources while men will engage more in very physical – what is often called rough-and-tumble – play (RTP) (Lamb and Lewis, 2014). As we suggested back in Chapter 6, rough-and-tumble play is considered to be a very important element in children's play repertoire (Flanders et al., 2009). Children rate this kind of play very highly and their choice of play partner for this would be their father according to research carried out in 1989 by Ross and Taylor. Almost 30 years later, van Polanen et al. (2017) assert that this is still the case and that through this kind of engagement 'men play a unique role in the development of children's autonomy and their openness to the outside world' (p. 414). Mothers may also be drawn more to engaging with the child in pretend play (described as play that 'involves some form of representation or acting-as-if, such that the behaviors or actions that take place in a pretend game are not meant to literally reflect reality' (Weisburg, 2015, p. 250)) than fathers are, because they value it more. Gleason (2005, cited in John et al., 2013, p. 484) suggests that this is because 'mothers view pretend play as educational, whereas fathers view pretend play as fun'.

TABLE 9.1 Linking anecdotal evidence about parents to literature

Example of interaction	Link to literature
Harry, a new father, takes three months shared parental leave (SPL) in addition to his paternity leave.	Sarkardi et al. (2008) set out how the fathering role has evolved 'from moral teacher and disciplinarian … to the new nurturing, coparenting-father' (p. 153).

Time to consider

Think about the parents that you know (not necessarily your own!) Now reflect on how they interact with their children. It might be within the domains of discipline, play and language, or you may be able to think of other significant areas of interaction. Can you find any research literature on gendered parental interactions? Completing a table like Table 9.1 may help you with your thoughts.

Are there differences in how mothers and fathers impact on their children's development?

If we acknowledge that there are differences in how mothers and fathers act with their children, then the next step is to consider whether there are differences in how they impact on their children's development. A useful place to start is a special issue of *Early Child Development and Care* from 2013. In the editorial, Newland et al. (2013) summarise some of the implications of mothering and fathering for children's development from the studies that make up the special edition. They recognise that there are differences in parenting styles which lead to differences in 'impacts on children's linguistic, social–emotional, and behavioural outcomes' (p. 339). Interestingly, although they state that there are similarities between mothers and fathers too, these are similarities in their involvement, not impact:

> In most studies, both mothers and fathers reported at least some involvement in caregiving but also some involvement in reading, playing, and roughhousing with their child. Within older samples, both parents also reported involvement in transporting their child to activities, assisting with homework, attending school events, etc. In addition, parents seem to be similarly responsive to children's needs, regardless of differences in interactional styles. Thus, while mothers and fathers may take on differential roles within families, roles oftentimes overlap, and parents balance their involvement with the day-to-day conditions of modern family life.
> (Newland et al., 2012, pp. 339–340)

In the following sections we are going to look at what the differences are in mothers' and fathers' impact on two areas of their children's development – (a) children's peer competence and pro-social behaviour and (b) their academic achievements.

Children's peer competence and pro-social behaviour

There are papers that have explored the literature on whether there are differences between how mothers and fathers impact on their children's development. For instance, the Fatherhood Institute (2013) considers which different roles mothers and fathers play in their children's attainments. And unlike Newland et al. (2013), the Fatherhood Institute (2013) are writing from a UK perspective. They state that one might assume that a mother's influence on their child's development would be greater than the father's because mothers 'still assume overriding responsibility for children's education'. However, their report highlights that there are contradictory pieces of research; some findings suggest mothers are more influential, and others that fathers have greater impact on their child's development. For instance, they cite Campbell and von Stauffenberg's findings (2008) that high levels of paternal sensitivity (i.e., how fathers recognise their children's needs and respond to them) impact on children's school readiness to a greater degree than maternal sensitivity. Campbell and von Stauffenberg (2008, p. 248) suggest that this shows that 'fathers make a unique contribution to the development of regulatory skills in young children' perhaps because 'fathers challenge their children in ways that especially facilitate adaption beyond the family circle and thus contribute to adjustment to school ... possibly via effects on peer competence and independence'. However, this is in part at odds with research from Lindsey et al. (2013) in the Mexican context. These researchers conducted videotaped observations of parents playing with their child individually when the child was approximately 18 months old. Then around 8 months later they observed the child in their ECEC setting; their findings are really interesting. The children of those mothers who displayed high levels of positive emotion during the videotaped observations demonstrated more pro-social behaviour at their ECEC setting. However, the children of fathers who displayed high levels of positive emotion demonstrated *less* pro-social behaviour with their peers. The researchers suggest that 'it may be overly expressive fathers, whether they may be displaying positive or negative emotion, model behaviour that is not conducive to children's development of pro-social behaviour with peers' (2013, p. 390).

Similarly, Jia et al. (2012, cited in Yogman and Garfield, 2016) have also explored parental impacts on children's social and emotional development. They found in their study that a high level of fathers' engagement with their preschool children's play led to the children displaying decreased 'externalizing and internalizing behaviour problems and enhanced social competence' (p. 5). In other words, fathers are supporting children's social and emotional development by playing with them as preschoolers. And there's a reason why many of the studies that explore fathers' involvement recruit children in the preschool period. Pleck (1983, cited in John et al., 2013) suggests that this is an important time to consider differences between mothers' and fathers' involvement, as fathers are likely to spend more time with their children when they reach early childhood than they did in infancy (p. 484). This continues as the children begin formal schooling; thus, their academic achievements are another important area to think about in terms of differences in parental impact.

Children's academic achievements

Another area where mothers and fathers may make a different contribution to their children's development is in the development of their literacy skills. Clarke (2009) looked at the role that fathers play in this important area; she cites an American paper by McBride et al. (2009) that looked at the differences between mothers' and fathers' parenting behaviours, their school involvement and the impact this had on their children's school achievement. They found that there were differences in how the mothers' and fathers' behaviours and interactions impacted on children's school success, suggesting that 'these findings lend support to the argument that fathers and mothers may assume different roles in raising their children, and these unique roles may have differential relationships with child outcomes such as student achievement' (McBride et al., 2009, p. 12).

They stress that this means readers should pay careful attention when reading studies about 'parental involvement', as often that implicitly means 'maternal involvement' (due to the sample of participants) and this study suggests that we need to be mindful of the differences between mothers' and fathers' involvement.

Time to consider

Within the EYFS there is the requirement that 'the key person must seek to engage and support parents and/or carers in guiding their child's development at home' (Department for Education, 2017, p. 10). If there is research that mothers and fathers impact on their children's development in different ways, some may argue practitioners should tailor their guidance according to whether they are engaging with the mother or father. Make a list of the reasons (and evidence) for and against this argument using a table like Table 9.2.

TABLE 9.2 Considering the argument for and against tailoring practitioner guidance based on parental gender

Statement: As mothers and fathers impact on their child's development in different ways, practitioners should tailor their guidance according to which parent they are engaging with.	
Arguments for:	Arguments against:

What tensions exist within the concepts of 'fathering' and 'mothering'?

There are some tensions that exist within the concepts of 'fathering' and 'mothering'. As we said earlier, the verbs 'to father' and 'to mother' can have different implications; furthermore, the more generic (and gender-neutral) term 'to parent', is also defined differently. Even if we are able to resolve these definitions, there are other tensions to consider; this is what we will do in this section of the chapter. The first area of contention we will explore is the moral panic around the need for 'father figures' and then we will reflect on some of the limitations that have been identified when conducting research on fathers and mothers.

The need for 'father figures'

The idea of males being role models to children in educational settings is a contested term but one that reoccurs frequently and is well documented in the research literature (Brownhill, 2014; Cushman, 2008; Mills et al., 2004; Wernersson, 2015). The argument most often discussed is that of the growing number of children living in one-parent families in the United Kingdom. The Office for National Statistics (2016) cites figures of 2.9 million lone parents with dependent children in the UK, the majority of which (86%) are headed by women (p. 5). This suggests that many children have no access to a 'father figure' in their daily lives and encouraging more men into the ECEC sector would address this deficit. The confusion around this debate arises from the fact that there is no clear definition of what a role model is, what dispositions and attitudes the role model is supposed to be demonstrating and how these are gender specific (Brownhill, 2014; Cushman, 2008). Men are also uncomfortable with being cast in this role and can see it as a 'burden' (Brownhill and Oates, 2016). Furthermore, this discourse risks presenting the 'lone mother' as inadequate; yet Golombok et al. (2016) assert that 'solo motherhood, in itself, does not result in psychological problems for children' (p. 409). We think we need to be clear here; if we say children *need* a father figure, we are making an assumption that what a mother is able to provide is not good enough. Likewise, we would like to challenge the notion that children *need* a mother figure, as Bowlby's (1953) now-outdated theory of maternal deprivation once suggested.

Certainly, there is a sense that those children being raised without a male father figure are at a disadvantage to those who benefit from interacting with such a figure on a regular basis. Although this is a contested viewpoint (Golombok, 2016) nevertheless it is this argument which underpins the moral panic surrounding the lack of men in ECEC. Indeed, it explains some of the rationale in government policy for recruiting male practitioners. The Department for Education's (2017, p. 24) Early Years Workforce Strategy states that in 2008 '17% of children from lone parent families had fewer than two hours a week of contact time with a man, whilst

36% had under six hours' and thus male ECEC practitioners are 'vital in making sure young children have quality contact time with men'. Yet at the same time Warin (2019, p. 295) draws on Tasker and Golombok's work (1997) to argue that 'there are no adverse outcomes for children brought up in lesbian-headed families with two same-sex female parents'. Warin continues to say their study 'concludes it is not fathers' maleness that matters but their role as an *additional* parent' (p. 295).

Conducting research on mothering and fathering

However, there has been some difficulty around research on fathering; most notably it has been carried out in a small-scale, qualitative way that relies on mothers as participants reporting on the behaviours and practices of the fathers (Bolshaw and Josephidou, 2018). This is something that Goldman and Burgess (2018) report for the Fatherhood Institute. They say that because fathers are less likely to be living with their child that their perspectives are often left out of research. Or, when information about fathers is gathered, it is through the perspectives of the child or the child's mother. Clarke (2009, p. 6) has also drawn attention to issues in the reliability and validity of research that has been conducted about fathers' involvement. She gives seven bullet points that must be considered:

- A lack of empirical studies, and lack of quantitative studies with adequate sample sizes, meaning that evidence on this issue is, to a large part, qualitative. Only rarely have studies investigated the robustness of father involvement by controlling for other variables, such as mother involvement, marital relationship, socio-economic status.
- Data are derived primarily from US studies, which raises issues with generalisation to the UK context.
- Data are mainly based on self-report, which raises issues of validity. There is ample evidence that parents may under- or over-report their level of involvement in something, such as child care. To make matters worse, the extent of father involvement is often based on the mother's report.
- Infrequent recourse to theoretical frameworks, although there are some well-known models (e.g. Lamb et al, 1985) that stress the multi-dimensionality of the father-involvement construct.
- Inconsistent operationalisation of father involvement (uni-dimensional vs. multi-dimensional) – linked to problems with definitions and results in potentially inconsistent results across studies.
- Inconsistent measurement of father involvement – for example, time spent together versus quality of the relationship. For a review see Allen and Daly (2007).
- Variations in outcome measures, i.e. different tests are used to measure an outcome variable such as literacy status or self-esteem.

Some of those bullet points might be a bit tricky to understand, so do spend some time reflecting on them. One bullet point that you might find problematic is that there is 'Infrequent recourse to theoretical frameworks'. What this means is that there is a lack of theoretical models that help us to understand fathers' involvement. Clarke (2009) also refers to some interesting research to back up these bullet points – for instance, that in a study by Mikelson (2008) mothers were found to underestimate by more than 10% how long fathers spend on activities with their children.

You might be wondering what the consequences of the limitations that Clarke (2009) identifies might be. According to the Fatherhood Institute, this means that when policy is developed it will not fully meet parents' and children's needs, as it is based on inaccurate and incomplete research findings (Goldman and Burgess, 2018, p. 3). To counter this, the Fatherhood Institute are developing a series of literature reviews about fathers and fatherhood that considers the research that has been conducted on this topic over the last 20 years. In 2018 they published a report called 'Where's the daddy?', which focuses specifically on fathers and father figures in the UK and what we know about them. In the report they examine how prevalent being a father figure is; almost 90% of 70-year-olds have fathered a child or played a significant role in a child's life (Speight et al., 2013).

Modern Fatherhood, a funded research collaboration, also think that more research is needed to help the development of policy. They are building a picture of contemporary fatherhood in the UK by analysing data from four large-scale surveys – Understanding Society, the European Union Labour Force Survey, the European Social Survey and the British Household Panel Study. They believe that doing research like this is important because it provides stronger evidence about fathers to help 'policy makers, employers and practitioners develop father friendly work-family policies and practices' and provide 'space for a conversation about men, families and work life' (Modern Fatherhood, 2018).

We do not want to leave research on mothers out, though. There is a really interesting qualitative longitudinal piece of research that has been conducted on motherhood called *The Making of Modern Motherhood* (Thomson et al., 2011). They collected their data through 131 questionnaires and 62 interviews with expectant mothers, and then 12 case studies. The case studies incorporated interviews with 'grandmothers, great-grandmothers and "significant others"' (Thomson et al., 2008, p. 6) with the aim of adding to research about how new mothers experience motherhood and what it means to their identities to be a mother. It also examines generational differences and similarities between pregnancy and motherhood. One of their interesting findings explores how first-time mothers of different ages experience their pregnancy. The younger interview participants (the youngest being 15) stood 'at the centre of familial dramas … and birth tended to be a collective affair involving mothers and friends as well as partners'; those in the 26–35-year-old age group spoke about 'the right moment' and 'settling down' while those in the older age group (the oldest participant was 48) spoke about their pregnancies as 'something that "almost did not happen", a "last chance", or "impossible dream"' (2008, p. 8).

Motherhood and fatherhood

Time to consider

Imagine you are a researcher in a position to conduct a piece of research about motherhood or fatherhood. What would your research question be? How would you attempt to find the answer to your question (i.e. what research methods would you use)? What literature can you find that already links to your area of interest?

Case study

Helin is a tutor working with work-based students who are training to be early years teachers. They all have many years working in ECEC settings and are very knowledgeable about practice. When Helin states that the following week's session is going to be about how to involve fathers, a lively discussion ensues. The students believe it is not appropriate to use the word 'father'; one of them suggests the word 'FUDGE' (fathers, uncles, dads, grandads and everyone) is a more appropriate term that they have adopted in their setting. Helin understands their point of view but cannot reconcile the fact that in this perspective a father seems to come lower in the hierarchy than a mother.

Possible solution

Helin reflects on what it means to fathers if they are not given the same level of importance as mothers as primary caregivers and are instead seen as comparable to 'everyone'. Yet at the same time, she knows from the Centre for Social Justice (2013, p. 3) that 'one million children have no meaningful contact at all with their fathers, and that's a conservative estimate' and so it is important to acknowledge the other men, including uncles, grandfathers and other family members and friends, that might be a part of children's lives in their place, including the children of her work-based students. She knows that she needs to consider this area sensitively but decides that she will talk to the students about using the term 'father figures' instead, as the Fatherhood Institute (2019) do. She thinks that such a term might better demonstrate that fathers, and those equal to them, share the same place in the hierarchy as mothers.

Final reflection

In this chapter we have considered some of the perceived differences in the ways that mothers and fathers engage with their children; we have looked in particular at the areas of play, language and discipline. Throughout the chapter, we have continually used the adjective 'perceived' to recognise that: (a) the research literature reveals contradictory findings and (b) the self-reporting, or indeed 'mother-reporting', in research data make the accompanying methodologies quite problematic. One prevalent fathering stereotype is the Victorian disciplinarian, but in fact there is research to suggest that fathers are just as sensitive as mothers; furthermore, mothers do not always agree that this is the case. We have also considered how mothers and fathers might have different impacts on their children's pro-social behaviour, peer competence and academic achievement and noted what the research literature suggests about this. The concepts of 'fathering' and 'mothering' bring with them many tensions; even by using these two terms we are returning to a binary discussion which we have encouraged you to try and avoid throughout this book. However, we make no apologies; these are very important areas of research to consider, particularly in relation to the negative discourses around single mothers and invisible fathers.

Key points

- There is research to suggest that mothers and fathers engage and interact with their children in different ways, particularly regarding discipline, play and language.
- In some areas, mothers and fathers have differing impacts on their child's development, for instance in relation to their peer competence, pro-social behaviours and academic attainment.
- Tensions exist between the concepts of motherhood and fatherhood. Part of these tensions can be explained by the moral panic about single mothers and the need for children to have a male 'role model'. Further tensions may be attributed to the fact that there are many limitations to research gathering fathers' perspectives, which may lead to policy oversights.

Further reading

1   Clarke, C. (2009) *Why fathers matter to their children's literacy.* Available from: https://literacytrust.org.uk/research-services/research-reports/why-fathers-matter-their-childrens-literacy-2009-review(accessed: 24th August, 2017).

   Have a look at a report written by Clarke (2009) on behalf of the Literacy Trust about the role that fathers play in their children's literacy. Bear in mind that it's a relatively old source, but think about what questions it raises for you.

2 Winsler, A., Madigan, A.L. and Aquilino, S.A. (2005) 'Correspondence between maternal and paternal parenting styles in early childhood', *Early Childhood Research Quarterly*, 20 (1), pp. 1–12.

It is worth having a read of Winsler et al.'s (2005) study about the similarities and differences in mothers' and fathers' parenting styles.

References

Bolshaw, P. and Josephidou, J. (2018) *Introducing Research in Early Childhood*. London: Sage.

Bowlby, J. (1953) *Child Care and the Growth of Love*. London: Penguin Books.

Brownhill, S. (2014) 'Build me a male role model!' A critical exploration of the perceived qualities/characteristics of men in the early years (0-8) in England', *Gender and Education*, 26(3), pp. 246–261.

Brownhill, S. and Oates, R. (2016) 'Who do you want me to be? An exploration of female and male perceptions of 'imposed' gender roles in the early years', *Education 3–13*, 45(5), pp. 658–670.

Campbell, S.B. and von Stauffenberg, C. (2008) 'Child characteristics and family processes that predict behavioral readiness for school', in: A. Booth and A.C. Crouter (eds) *Disparities in School Readiness: How do Families Contribute to Transitions into School?* pp. 225–258. New York: Lawrence Erlbaum Associates.

The Centre for Social Justice (2013) *Fractured Families: Why Stability Matters*. Available at: www.centreforsocialjustice.org.uk/core/wp-content/uploads/2016/08/CSJ_Fractured_Families_Report_WEB_13.06.13-1.pdf (accessed: 19th August 2019).

Clarke, C. (2009) *Why Fathers Matter to their Children's Literacy*. Available from: www.literacytrust.org.uk/assets/0000/0770/Father_review_2009.pdf (accessed 24th August 2019).

Cushman, P. (2008) 'So what exactly do you want? What principals mean when they say "male role model"', *Gender and Education*, 20(2), pp. 123–136.

Department for Education (2017) *Early Years Workforce Strategy*. Available at: https://assets.publishing.service.gov.uk/government/uploads/system/uploads/attachment_data/file/596884/Workforce_strategy_02-03-2017.pdf (accessed: 19th August 2019).

Fagan, J., Day, R., Lamb, M. and Cabrera, N. (2014) 'Should researchers conceptualize differently the dimensions of parenting for fathers and mothers?', *Journal of Family Theory and Review*, 6(4), pp. 390–405.

Fatherhood Institute (2013) *Fatherhood Institute Research Summary: Fathers' Impact on their Children's Learning and Achievement*. Available at: www.fatherhoodinstitute.org/2013/fatherhood-institute-research-summary-fathers-and-their-childrens-education/(accessed: 19th August 2019).

Fatherhood Institute (2019) *About Us*. Available at: www.fatherhoodinstitute.org/about-the-fatherhood-institute/(accessed: 19th August 2019).

Flanders, J.L., Leo, V., Paquette, D., Pihl, R.O. and Seguin, J.R. (2009) 'Rough-and-tumble play and the regulation of aggression: An observational study of Father–child play dyads', *Aggressive Behaviour*, 35(4), pp. 285–295.

Goldman, R. and Burgess, A. (2018) *Where's the Daddy? Fathers and Father-Figures in UK Datasets*. Available at: www.fatherhoodinstitute.org/wp-content/uploads/2017/12/Wheres-the-daddy-Executive-Summary-3.pdf (accessed: 19th August 2019).

Golombok, S., Zadeh, S., Imrie, S., Smith, V. and Freeman, T. (2016) 'Single mothers by choice: Mother–child relationships and children's psychological adjustment', *Journal of Family Psychology*, 30(4), pp. 409–418.

John, A., Halliburton, A. and Humphrey, J. (2013) 'Child–mother and child–father play interaction patterns with preschoolers', *Early Child Development and Care*, 183 (3–4), pp. 483–497.

Lamb, M.E. (2000) 'The history of research on father involvement: an overview', *Marriage and Family Review*, 29(2–3), pp. 23–42.

Lamb, M.E. (ed) (2010) *The Role of the Father in Child Development*, 5th edn. New York, NY: Wiley.

Lamb, M.E. and Lewis, C. (2014) 'Father child relationships', in: N.J. Cabrera and C.S. Tamis-Lemonda (eds) *Handbook of Father Involvement: Multidisciplinary Perspectives*, 2nd. Hove: Routledge.

Lindsey, E.W., Caldera, Y.M. and Rivera, M. (2013) 'Mother–child and father–child emotional expressiveness in Mexican-American families and toddlers' peer interactions', *Early Child Development and Care*, 183(3–4), pp. 378–393.

London Early Years Foundation (2012) *Men Working in Childcare: Does It Matter to Children? What do they say?* Available at: www.leyf.org.uk/wp-content/uploads/2018/06/Men-in-Childcare-Version-141112.pdf (accessed: 31st May 2019).

McBride, B.A., Dyer, W.J., Liu, Y., Brown, G.L. and Hong, S. (2009) 'The differential impact of early father and mother involvement on later student achievement', *Journal of Educational Psychology*, 101, pp. 498–508.

Mikelson, K.S. (2008) 'He said, she said: comparing mother and father reports of father involvement', *Journal of Marriage and Family*, 70(3), pp. 613–624.

Mills, M., Martino, W. and Lingard, B. (2004) 'Attracting, recruiting and retaining male teachers: policy issues in the male teacher debate', *British Journal of Sociology of Education*, 25, pp. 355–368.

Modern Fatherhood. (2018) *Modern Fatherhood*. Available at: www.modernfatherhood.org (accessed: 19th August 2019).

Marshall, D., Davis, T., Hogg, M.K., Schneider, T. and Petersen, A. (2014) 'From overt provider to invisible presence: discursive shifts in advertising portrayals of the father in Good Housekeeping, 1950-2010', *Journal of Marketing Management*, 30(15;16), pp. 1654–1679.

Newland, L.A., Coyl-Shepherd, D.D. and Paquette, D. (2013) 'Implications of mothering and fathering for children's development', *Early Child Development and Care*, 183 (3–4), pp. 337–342.

Office for National Statistics (2016) *Statistical Bulletin: Families and Households in the UK: 2016*. Available from: www.ons.gov.uk/peoplepopulationandcommunity/birthsdeathsandmarriages/families/bulletins/familiesandhouseholds/2016 (accessed: 19th August 2019).

Pancsofar, N. and Vernon-Feagans, L. (2006) 'Mother and father language input to young children: contributions to later language development', *Journal of Applied Developmental Psychology*, 27(6), pp. 571–587.

Raeburn, P. (2014) *Do Fathers Matter?* New York: Macmillan.

Ross, H. and Taylor, H. (1989) 'Do boys prefer daddy or his physical style of play', *Sex Roles*, 20, pp. 23–33.

Sarkardi, A., Kristiansson, R., Oberklaid, F. and Bremberg, S. (2008) 'Fathers' involvement and children's developmental outcomes: a systematic review of longitudinal studies', *Acta Peadiatrica*, 97(2), pp. 153–158.

Speight, S., Poole, E., O'Brien, M., Connolly, S. and Aldrich, M. (2013) *Men and fatherhood: Who are today's fathers?* Available at: www.modernfatherhood.org/wp-content/uploads/2013/05/Pages-from-Who-are-todays-fathers.pdf (accessed: 19th August 2019).

Tasker, F. and Golombok, S. (1997) *Growing Up in a Lesbian Family: Effects on Child Development.* New York: Guilford Press.

Thomson, R. and Kehily, M.J. with Hadfield, L. and Sharpe, S. (2008) *The Making of Modern Motherhood: Memories, Representations and Practices.* Available at: www3.open.ac.uk/events/0/200873_43860_o1.pdf (accessed: 19th August 2019).

Thomson, R., Kehily, M.J., Hadfield, L. and Sharpe, S. (2011) *Making Modern Mothers.* Bristol: The Policy Press.

van Polanen, M., Colonnesi, C., Tavecchio, L.W.C., Blokhuis, S. and Fukkink, R.G. (2017) 'Men and women in childcare: A study of caregiver-child interactions', *European Early Childhood Educaiton Researh Journal*, 25(3), pp. 412–424. doi: 10.1080/1350293X.2017.1308165.

Warin, J. (2019) 'Conceptualising the value of male practitioners in early childhood education and care: gender balance or gender flexibility', *Gender and Education*, 31(3), pp. 293–308. doi: 10.1080/09540253.2017.1380172.

Weisburg, D.S. (2015) 'Pretend play', *WIREs Cognitive Science*, 6(2), pp. 249–261.

Wernersson, I. (2015) 'Missing men' in Swedish ECE and care' in: S. Brownhill, J. Warin and I. Wernersson (eds) *Men, Masculinities and Teaching in Early Childhood Education: International Perspectives on Gender and Care.* Oxon: Routledge.

Winsler, A., Madigan, A.L. and Aquilino, S.A. (2005) 'Correspondence between maternal and paternal parenting styles in early childhood', *Early Childhood Research Quarterly*, 20(1), pp. 1–12.

Yogman, M. and Garfield, C.F. (2016) 'Fathers' roles in the care and development of their children: the role of pediatricians', *American Academy of Pediatrics Clinical Report*, 138(1). Available at: http://pediatrics.aappublications.org/content/pediatrics/early/2016/06/10/peds.2016-1128.full.pdf (accessed: 19th August 2019).

CHAPTER

Gender issues in health

Are there any differences?

Introduction

For the final chapter in this part of the book we thought it would be both interesting and relevant to consider if there were any gendered health issues that it would be important for an early years practitioner to be aware of. Take a moment to reflect on what you know about children's health in the UK. News organisations often share headlines around two areas in particular – young children's weight and their mental health difficulties. In 2018, a BBC News headline proclaimed: 'Record number of severely obese children'. In 2019, The Children's Society's 8th annual 'Good childhood report' shared statistics that children were the least happy they'd been since their first wave of data in 2009. If you regularly read the news then it's likely that neither of these headlines surprises you. But what about children who live outside the context of the UK? You might have come across reports by international organisations like the World Health Organisation (2018) that state: 'A child under 15 dies every 5 seconds around the world'. So, there are many sources which inform us about the state of children's health both in the UK and beyond but can we learn anything about the gendered differences in children's health outcomes? In this chapter we will:

- build your understanding of gendered differences in health outcomes for children,
- explore how inequality for girls also impacts negatively on boys,
- highlight gendered mental health issues and how they relate to early childhood.

This chapter will look beyond educational settings to explore whether there are gender differences in children's health outcomes, including the two-year-old check, the Early Learning Goal for physical development, rates of children's accidents, how likely girls and boys are to have an unhealthy weight and also their emotional health. It will consider what might explain these differences and what parents and practitioners need to be aware of in terms of children's trajectories, stressing that both boys and girls can suffer from the negative impact of hegemonic (Connell, 2005) masculinities.

What are the gendered differences in physical health outcomes for children?

We are going to ask a big question now – how long are you expecting to live? You have probably heard the statistics that women have a longer life expectancy than men. But to start this section, we want to share a quotation with you from Cheung (2018, p. 2):

> A boy born in the UK in 2015 can expect to live to just over 79 years; over a year longer than a boy born in Portugal, but more than a year less than one born in Sweden. The UK life expectancy for a boy is broadly similar to most European comparators. However, a girl born in the UK can expect to live to almost 83 years; three years less than a girl born in Spain, and the lowest of all European comparators. For both boys and girls, improvement in life expectancy has plateaued since 2011.

This is saying two important things. Firstly, there's inequality in terms of boys' and girls' life spans. We'll consider one of the reasons for this a little later. Secondly, while the life expectancy for males born in the UK in 2018 is comparable for boys across Europe, for girls born in the UK it's not looking as good – their life expectancy is the lowest of their counterparts across Europe. So, what is happening across their lifespan to create this inequality? And what could we be doing specifically when children are in early childhood to try and prevent the disparity in boys' and girls' life expectancy outcomes? In this section we are first going to look at what's happening in high-income countries and then we are going to think about what's happening in the majority world.

In high-income countries

Let's start by thinking about gendered health differences when children are born. As we said in Chapter 3 (Does a child's gender impact on how they learn?), when children are born their weight, length and head circumference are tracked on different growth charts, depending on whether they are girls or boys (RCPH, 2013). Therefore, we know from the very beginning of a child's life that there are physical differences (apart from the obvious anatomical ones) depending on sex. Boys are born with a stronger grasp and a tendency to be more active (Fausto-Sterling et al., 2012). They have greater leg strength at three months, greater arm strength at nine months, yet less ability at birth to control their motor functions (Fausto-Sterling et al., 2012). Girls have greater resistance to infection (Sidebotham, 2014), which may contribute to the lower mortality rate among girls compared to boys. And on average boys are born half a pound heavier than girls, although differences in weight diminish and have disappeared by the time children are between two and three years old (Fausto-Sterling et al., 2012).

Yet as we said in the introduction, one area that is often discussed with regard to children's physical health is their weight. Statistics from 2019 report that at age four to five, 10% of boys and 9% of girls are obese (Baker, 2019). Those percentages are pretty similar. Yet by age 10 to 11, 22% of boys and 18% of girls are obese. Does this surprise you? What might explain this difference? You might think that it's a difference in the amount of exercise that children are undertaking. Sport England (2018) have analysed data from over 130,000 children aged between 5 and 16 and have found that 'boys (20%) are more likely to be active every day than girls (14%). The gap between boys and girls who are active every day is wider from Years 5–6 (ages 9–11) upwards' (p. 6). However, Farooq et al. (2018) have analysed data from the Millennium Cohort Study and suggest that although the amount of physical activity that boys and girls do declines throughout childhood and adolescence, there isn't a marked difference between girls and boys. They therefore suggest that 'we should abandon the concept of "high risk groups" (e.g., adolescent girls) for low physical activity – [because] most of the paediatric population is at high risk' (2018, p. 6). Yet Farooq et al.'s (2018) findings are at odds with that of other research – for instance, that conducted by The World Health Organisation (2016). They published a report called 'Growing up unequal: Gender and socioeconomic differences in young people's health and well-being'. They report that there are differences in how many boys and girls report at least 60 minutes of moderate-to-vigorous physical activity per day at ages 11, 13 and 15 in England, which echo that of the other 41 countries that were part of the research. They suggest that 'girls should be targeted with gender-sensitive approaches and interventions' (2016, p. 143). What do you think? Should both boys and girls be targeted to support them in maintaining a sufficient amount of physical activity? Or is it appropriate to aim interventions specifically at girls?

The research conducted by Farooq et al. (2018) and the World Health Organisation (2016) both investigated the physical activity of teenagers, so we need here to look back to see what is happening with younger children and their physical development. If we look at the EYFS Profile results for 2018 we can see that girls outperform boys in all of the Early Learning Goals (ELGs) although the gap between boys and girls outcomes is narrowing (Department for Education, 2018). For the ELGs that relate specifically to Physical Development, Moving and Handling, and Health and Self-Care, there is an 8.9% and 6.3% difference in the percentage of boys and girls who achieve these goals, in favour of girls. Therefore, this certainly doesn't suggest that practice and pedagogy in ECEC settings is priming girls to be less confident in their physical abilities as they grow up. And although there is a common stereotype that baby boys might hit their physical developmental milestones quicker than girls, one study has found there's no evidence that this is the case. A longitudinal piece of research conducted across five countries (Ghana, India, Norway, Oman and the USA) found that there were no differences in when boys and girls reached milestones in six areas of gross motor development – 'sitting without support, hands-and-knees crawling, standing with assistance, walking with assistance, standing alone, and walking alone' (WHO Multicentre Growth References Study Group, 2006. p. 66). Yet mothers typically underestimate their infant daughters' gross motor skills and overestimate their sons' efforts (Mondschein et al., 2000).

After early childhood, differences do appear in children's gross motor skills. Studies have shown how boys can run faster, jump higher and throw further; they also develop the ability to do more advanced forms of kicking, catching and throwing at earlier ages than girls, too (Mondschein et al., 2000). You might wonder if these gendered differences in growth and physical development lead to differences in the rates of accidents that boys and girls have. There are notable differences, which is why The Royal College of Paediatrics and Child Health (2017) have stated in a report called 'State of child health' that 'safe play, home, and outdoor environments are vital, as injuries still account for a large proportion of the mortality burden, particularly in boys' (p. 22). From the age of one, injury is the most common reason for death in childhood and adolescence; for instance, unintentional injuries as a result of traffic accidents and drowning, as well as intentional injuries like assault, self-harm and suicide (Wolfe et al., 2014, p. 12). These types of external cause of death (in contrast to other types, like cancer, infection or congenital conditions) are higher in boys than girls at all ages. In early and middle childhood, Sidebotham et al. (2014) argue that there might be a link between external causes and other biological and social effects. And in adolescence they suggest this might be because of higher levels of risk-taking and aggression (Sidebotham et al. (2014). Indeed, the World Health Organisation (2016) report that in children aged 11–15 'boys are involved in fighting more often at all ages and are significantly more likely to be perpetrators of bullying' (p. 238). Others have linked the gendered differences in accident rates and suicide to differences in motor development (Pinker, 2008, cited in Fausto-Sterling et al., 2012). Boys may make more errors than girls in their motor decisions, leading to more accidents (Plumert, 1997, cited in Mondschein et al., 2000).

In the majority world

While the World Health Organisation (2016) and Sidebotham et al. (2014) have focussed on gendered health differences in high-income countries, other organisations have looked at health-related gender inequality beyond this context. For instance, Unicef (2011) have produced a really interesting report on 'sex-disaggregated data on a selection of well-being indicators, from early childhood to young adulthood' (p. 1). What is interesting is that they note that there are no significant differences in outcomes for children within the early childhood range. They state that boys and girls are just as likely to have their birth registered, be breastfed, be undernourished, receive treatment via malaria interventions, or to have suspected pneumonia and diarrhoea. They are just as likely to receive violent discipline and attend preschool. Yet when children approach middle childhood and adolescence, differences become apparent, particularly with regard to attendance rates in secondary school. In South Asia girls are less likely to attend school, while the opposite is true in Latin America and the Caribbean. And when children approach late adolescence and young adulthood (from age 14) the discrepancies in gendered health outcomes become starker. For example, girls are more likely to be married as children and bear children themselves; this can lead to physical health complications as their young bodies are not prepared. Furthermore, girls are less likely to have comprehensive, accurate knowledge about HIV/AIDS, which is why 'young women in sub-Saharan Africa are two to four times more likely to be infected with HIV/AIDS than young men' (2011, p. 20).

Plan International (2016) have also produced a report on the links between gender inequality and early childhood development, but the picture they paint is not as positive as that of Unicef (2011). While they agree with Unicef that data across the world implies that there are no gendered health differences in early childhood (described as being aged between birth and four years), in some areas these do exist, particularly in areas with 'son preference'; that is, where sons are preferred to daughters for economic, religious and social reasons. For instance, with regard to feeding practices, often the males eat first so get the best nutrients and most protein. And in some places (for example, Egypt, Morocco, India and sub-Saharan Africa) girls are weaned off breastmilk earlier than boys. This is because breastfeeding is seen as a method of contraception, so stopping breastfeeding means that mothers may become pregnant sooner, hoping for a son (2016, p. 17). Plan International (2016) suggest that early childhood development programmes are important for tackling gender inequality, for example because they can improve children's health, nutrition and development, challenge gendered social norms and promote fathers to take a role in childrearing.

Time to consider

In total, Plan International (2016) give six reasons why early childhood development (ECD) programmes are important for tackling gender inequality and discrimination. Reflect on these and think what actions could be taken to achieve each of these statements:

> E.1 Comprehensive ECD programming that ensures a child receives adequate care, supports and services during the Early Years, is essential for her development and long-term well-being.
>
> E.2 ECD programmes are a great 'equaliser', capable of closing gaps between disadvantaged children and their more privileged peers.

E.3 ECD programmes offer a key opportunity to work with parents, caregivers, educators and communities to reflect on and transform gendered norms and early gender socialisation processes.

E.4 ECD programming also benefits older female siblings.

E.5 Mothers benefit from the provision of comprehensive ECD programmes

E.6 ECD programmes offer an entry point to promote reflection on attitudes, norms and expectations for men and women regarding care work and childrearing, and to promote male engagement with childcare and development – with benefits for all the family.

(Plan International, 2016, pp. 23–24)

What are the gendered differences in mental disorders for children?

In November 2018, the UK's Women and Equalities Committee within Parliament launched an inquiry into the mental health of men and boys, because of the concern about mental health problems in males and because 'still too little is known about what affects mental health for men and boys, the social and economic costs, the groups of men and boys that are most at risk and, most importantly, the action needed to tackle it' (Women and Equalities Committee, 2018). They invited submissions of evidence and received one from the Children and Young People's Mental Health Coalition (CYPMHC) (2019) who 'represents the views of over 180 of the leading charities, academic institutions and professional bodies who come together to campaign for the better mental health of infants, children and young people'. CYPMHC cite some information from the NHS (2018a) about children's mental health from a survey conducted with a sample of just over 9000 children aged between two and 19. The report is called 'Mental health of children and young people in England', 2017, and it categorises mental disorders into four key groups:

1. Emotional disorders,
2. Behavioural (or conduct) disorders,
3. Hyperactivity disorders,
4. Other less common disorders (including ASD, eating disorders, tic disorders).

It might surprise you that ASD (i.e. autism) is categorised by the NHS (2018a) as a mental disorder. When we think of mental disorders we often think of mental *ill* health and conditions like anxiety, depression and eating disorders. Yet all of the conditions within the NHS's report have been identified as mental disorders 'according to International Classification of Diseases (ICD-10) standardized diagnostic criteria, using the Development and Well-being Assessment

(DAWBA)' (2018a, p. 6). This doesn't mean that those with autism have mental ill health, but instead they have a developmental disorder (note that the 'D' in 'ASD' does itself stand for 'disorder'). It is for this reason that later in this section we talk about gendered differences in the diagnosis of autism, although we want to be clear that we recognize that autism is not a mental illness.

From the NHS (2018a) research, some of their key findings were:

- One in 18 children aged between two and four had been diagnosed with at least one mental disorder. A higher percentage of boys than girls had been diagnosed – 6.8% of boys in comparison with 4.2% of girls.
- One in ten children aged between five and ten had been diagnosed with at least one mental disorder. Almost double the amount of boys than girls had been diagnosed – 6.8% of boys in comparison with 4.2% of girls.
- One in seven children aged between 11 and 16 had at least one mental disorder. A very slightly higher percentage of girls than boys had been diagnosed – 14.3% of boys and 14.4% of girls.
- One in six children aged between 17 and 19 had at least one mental disorder. More than double the amount of girls than boys had been diagnosed – 10.3% of boys in comparison to 23.9% of girls.

Take a moment to look at the figures above. The statistics show that while at a young age (i.e. between two and ten) more boys than girls have diagnoses of mental disorders, by 17 more than twice the number of girls than boys had been diagnosed. What do you think that could imply? Do you think it means that boys aged two to four are more likely than girls of the same age to have a mental health condition? Do you think that boys have fewer mental health problems than girls as they approach adolescence and early childhood? The key word to bear in mind is 'diagnosed'. The NHS statistics aren't telling us how many children *have* mental health disorders, they are telling us how many are *diagnosed* with these conditions. Therefore, the disparities in the percentages of diagnoses imply that some children are going untreated and their conditions possibly unmanaged.

Let us look now at what types of conditions are diagnosed in children in the youngest age category of two to four years. The most commonly diagnosed disorders are behavioural (typically oppositional defiant disorder and autistic spectrum disorder (ASD)), and sleeping and feeding disorders (NHS, 2018a). Behavioural disorders are the most frequently diagnosed in children aged five to ten, followed by emotional disorders. The percentages of diagnoses for boys and girls with emotional disorders in this age range are quite similar. But for other types of disorders there are big differences in rates of diagnoses – for instance 2.6% of boys were diagnosed with hyperactivity disorder in comparison with just 0.8% of girls. Why do you think this might be?

Why the difference in rates of diagnoses?

One behavioural condition with a big difference in the number of boys and girls diagnosed is ASD. It's believed that the ratio of boys to girls with autism is 3:1 (Loomes et al., 2017) and there is a variety of theories that might explain the disparity in diagnosis rates (National Autistic Society, 2018). One reason suggested is that the clinical tools used to make diagnoses are based on how males with autism present, which leads to under-diagnosis in females. To counter this issue, it has been argued that diagnostic questions should be changed so that girls with autism are not overlooked (Gould and Ashton-Smith, 2011). Another reason for this difficulty is the fact that girls are better at 'camouflaging'; this means they mask their symptoms better than boys, because girls with autism are more likely to display 'compensatory behaviours, such as staying in close proximity to peers and weaving in and out of activities, which appeared to mask their social challenges' while boys tend to play alone (Dean et al., 2017, p. 678). It is for this reason that the charity nasen (which stands for the National Association of Special Educational Needs) talk of girls with autism 'flying under the radar' (2016, p. 1) because their behaviour does not align to traits stereotypically seen as being characteristics of those with ASD.

While boys are more likely to be diagnosed with ASD than girls, for emotional disorders the opposite is true. For children aged between 11 and 16, 10.9% of girls and 7.1% of boys were diagnosed with an emotional disorder (NHS, 2018a). For those aged between 17 and 19, 22.4% of girls and 7.9% of boys had an emotional disorder; this implies that boys are being under-diagnosed and may be in need of support and treatment. Boys and men may feel they need to conform to the stereotype that they are 'strong' and 'brave' and should not show emotion. Giving evidence for the Women and Equalities Committee's inquiry into the mental health of men and boys, Lee Cambule, a mental health campaigner, stated:

> There is this perception of men that they should be able to man up, get on with it and be strong in the face of that adversity. That then makes it difficult for them to open up and seek help and support. Whatever the trigger is, a lot of the things about being a man or a boy in that situation just make it more difficult to reach out and get the help you need.
> (Women and Equalities Committee, 2019).

Think back to the case study we considered in Chapter 1 (Introduction: Still talking about gender?), where a student on placement in an early years setting had overheard a practitioner saying 'Don't cry, you are a big boy'. From a very young age children may be hearing messages that boys need to 'man up' and hide their emotions. Yet one of the EYFS's Early Learning Goals, regarding 'Managing Feelings and Behaviour' requires children to 'talk about how they and others show feelings' (Early Education, 2012, p. 14). In 2018, 9.5% more girls than boys achieved this Early Learning Goal (Department for Education, 2018). This is an improvement from the 2012 EYFS Profile results (when the EYFS was revised) in which there was a 12% difference in the amount of boys and girls achieving the 'Managing Feelings and Behaviour' ELG. (Department for Education, 2013, p. 6). Yet it shows there is work to be done to support boys in particular to understand and manage their feelings and emotions.

Gender-sensitive approaches

It's been recognised elsewhere, too, that boys can have more difficulties in talking about their feelings, which is why a gender-sensitive approach is important. Gender-sensitive approaches in mental health support have been described as those which:

- undertake gender-specific work for specific groups,
- respond to the gendered ways that boys and girls experience mental health conditions,
- facilitate children to think about what role their gender plays in their health and well-being.

(Hamblin and Young, 2017, p. 5)

Hamblin and Young (2017) share the case study of Julie Berentsen, a mindfulness educator. She supports children in 'paying more attention to the present moment – to your own thoughts and feelings, and to the world around you' (NHS, 2018b). She runs a project in an inner-city school in London for children aged between five and ten, where she leads 30-minute sessions to promote the children's mindfulness and to respond to social and emotional needs such as well-being, anxiety and self-regulation. She identified that when she was delivering her weekly sessions, the boys struggled more than the girls in talking as part of a group. She realised that she had to take a gender-sensitive approach and recognise that the needs of the boys and the girls in the group were different. So she began to work with them on an individual basis at first, which then built up to pair-work and then finally talking in groups. Julie has had to challenge her inherited views about gender and be a continuously reflective practitioner, but by acting in this way she has enabled boys to develop the confidence to talk about their emotions in a safe, trusting environment.

This gender-sensitive approach is in contrast to a 'gender-blind' one. Gender blindness is the act of not recognising that boys and girls have different needs to each other. Unicef (2017, p. 3) describes it as:

> failure to recognise that the roles and responsibilities of men/boys and women/girls are given to them in specific social, cultural, economic and political contexts and backgrounds. Projects, programmes, policies and

TABLE 10.1 Identifying features of effective gender-sensitive approaches

Case study	Features of an effective gender-sensitive approach
E.g. Julie Berentsen, Mindfulness educator	E.g. Identifying that the boys and girls have different needs.
	E.g. Building up a trusting relationship with the children.
	E.g. Reflecting on own engrained beliefs about gender.

attitudes which are gender-blind do not take into account these different roles and diverse needs, maintain the status quo and will not help transform the unequal structure of gender relations.

Time to consider

Have a look at the report by Hamblin and Young (2017), published by the National Children's Bureau. It's available online. It shares a range of case studies of gender-sensitive approaches to supporting children's mental health, including the case of Julie Berentsen's mindfulness workshops and a case study about *CALMzine*, which we are discussing in the next section. When reading the case studies, make a note of what the features seem to be of effective gender-sensitive approaches. Using a table like Table 10.1 might help you.

Hamblin, E. and Young, H. (2017) *Gender-sensitive approaches to addressing children and young people's emotional and mental health and well-being*. London: National Children's Bureau. Available at: https://ncb.org.uk/sites/default/files/field/attachment/NCB%20-%20Examples%20of%20gender-sensitive%20practice%20with%20CYP%20-%20Aug%202017.pdf (accessed: 28th August 2019).

The impact of hegemonic masculinities

In Chapter 1 we introduced you to Connell (2005) and her comments on sex role theory, a theory which suggests we all conform to a general set of expectations because of the sex role attached to our gender. In Chapter 5 (Why is there a gender imbalance in the early years workforce?) we looked further at her work by signposting a 'thinking-about-gender' continuum. Here we will revisit Connell by introducing a 'framework of masculinities'; such a framework, suggested by Connell, can help us understand how men (and therefore boys) practice their gender or are positioned by others as they practice their gender.

If you look at Table 10.2 you can see that men deemed 'subordinate' are those that demonstrate stereotypically feminine traits. This belief doesn't just damage how women are seen (with their 'subordinate' traits) but it damages men's mental health too. As we said earlier, boys are told not to cry and to 'man up'.

> **Theorist in focus: Connell's (2005) masculinities**
>
> Connell (2005) provides a useful theoretical perspective in this framework that can be helpful in terms thinking about the roles boys may feel are open to them as they grow up. It is important to remember that Connell emphasises how much this is context-dependent, that it is a dynamic framework and therefore can never be used in a simple kind of sorting exercise. It does help us, however, to think about certain behaviours.
>
> **TABLE 10.2** Connell's (2005) Framework of Masculinities (adapted from Josephidou, 2017)
>
> | | |
> |---|---|
> | Hegemonic | Men who are defined as the 'definitive man' by their particular culture. |
> | Subordinate | Men who demonstrate character traits and dispositions normally associated with females (such as being emotional or prone to tears). |
> | Complicit | Men who don't 'meet the normative standards' (Connell, 2005, p. 79) to be a hegemonic male but benefit from it. These might be more likely to adopt a gender-blind approach. |
> | Marginalised | Men who are marginalised because of their class, race or sexuality by their particular culture. |

Comedian and author Robert Webb (2017), in his memoir *How Not to Be a Boy*, shares 'rules for being a man' which include 'don't cry, love sports, play rough, drink beer, don't talk about feelings'. The implications of this are that boys are socialised that to be 'the definitive man' they shouldn't express emotions or become upset. And the impact of this is that the boys grow up to be men with poor mental health. The Campaign Against Living Miserably (CALM) report that 'suicide is the single biggest killer of men under 45 in the UK' (CALM, 2018, p. 4). Seventy-five per cent of people who commit suicide in the UK are male (CALM, 2019). Hamblin and Young (2017) share a case study of a magazine produced by CALM, called *CALMzine*, which they describe as a gender-sensitive approach to

> 'address issues and ask questions about what's expected of young men in the 21st century, taking a nonclinical, non-aspirational approach that empowers young men to help themselves and each other. *CALMzine* allows men to express what they feel, and challenge unhelpful stereotypes about masculinity'
>
> (2017, p. 14).

Essentially, it is encouraging the challenging of hegemonic masculinities because they are damaging to both boys and girls.

As we consider these different ways of viewing masculinity, being those who work with young children, we must remind ourselves that these ideas can have a negative impact on the mental health of both girls *and* boys. If it is seen as lesser, weak or 'subordinate' to demonstrate feelings, we may teach children to hide them; this consequence is harmful to a happy, mindful society.

Time to consider

CALMzine is one strategy that the Campaign Against Living Miserably (CALM) have implemented to provide support for men at risk of suicide. Can you make a list of other gender-sensitive strategies you are aware of that supports mental health?

Case study

Ivan is working in a preschool room. He has noticed that there isn't a big difference between the number of girls and boys that are overweight. Yet one of his friends works in a primary school and says that there is a greater number of boys that are overweight than girls by the time they finish primary school. He wonders what strategies could help boys and girls maintain healthy weights.

Possible response

Ivan decides to do some reading about children's levels of activity, as he believes there will be a link between this and their weight. He reads Farooq et al.'s (2018) findings that the amount of physical activity that children engage in reduces as they grow up, along with their recommendation that 'Future efforts to arrest age-related decline in physical activity should begin well before adolescence' (2018, p. 5). He also reflects on his knowledge of the differences between taking a gender-sensitive or gender-blind approach. He decides that a gender-sensitive approach that takes into account the girls' and boys' differing attitudes to physical activity and their weight would be more appropriate. He plans to do some reading about what a gender-sensitive approach might look like in practice.

Final reflection

This chapter considered what the gendered differences are in children's physical health and their mental health. It looked at how differences in children's physical health vary depending on where a child is growing up. We have also seen how rates of diagnoses of some mental disorders in children differ dramatically between girls and boys. But that doesn't mean that the actual number of children with these disorders necessarily differs to such a degree – it might mean that some boys and girls are going undiagnosed. And if we challenge the idea that boys have to be 'big and strong' (hegemonic) in our work with young children, we might impact on the number of both boys and girls that suffer from mental health problems both as young children and then as they grow older.

Key points

- There are gendered differences in children's physical health, both in high-income countries and in the majority world. Many of these differences do not emerge until middle childhood and adolescence; there are limited gendered differences in children's physical health in early childhood.
- There are gendered differences in children's mental health. Boys are more likely to be diagnosed with ASD; girls are more likely to be diagnosed with emotional disorders. Effective diagnostic tools and gender-sensitive approaches are necessary to ensure that children's mental health and well-being needs are met.
- Both boys' and girls' mental health may be impacted as the result of hegemonic (Connell, 2005) masculinities (Anderson, 2012). It's important to challenge ideas around these in order to counter gendered health inequalities for both boys and girls and to reduce male suicide rates. Organisations like CALM are a good starting point for talking about the 'ways to be a man' and for addressing the issue of male suicide.

Further reading

1. Unicef (2011) *Boys and girls in the life cycle: Sex-disaggregated data on a selection of well-being indicators, from early childhood to young adulthood*. New York: United Nations Children's Fund. Available at: https://unicef.org/media/files/Gender_hi_res.pdf (accessed: 28th August 2019).

    This report examines statistics to consider the differences in boys' and girls' health, well-being and education outcomes in the majority world. It's an accessible read and it is interesting to reflect on where the gendered differences lie.

2. nasen (2015) *Girls and autism: Flying under the radar*. Staffordshire: nasen. Available at: http://nasen.org.uk/resources/resources.girls-and-autism-flying-under-the-radar.html (accessed: 28th August 2019).

    This is a really lovely report which identifies the issues around girls with ASD. There's a very helpful table which outlines strategies for those working with girls with autism in educational settings.

References

Anderson, E. (2012) *Inclusive Masculinity: The Changing Nature of Masculinities*. Oxon: Routledge.

Baker, C. (2019) *Briefing Paper: Obesity Statistics*. Available at: https://researchbriefings.parliament.uk/ResearchBriefing/Summary/SN03336#fullreport (accessed: 29th August 2019).

BBC News (2018) *Record Number of Severely Obese Children*. Available at: https://bbc.co.uk/news/health-44926893 (accessed: 28th August 2019).

Campaign for Living Miserably (CALM (2018) *CALM Greatest Hits 2017-18*. Available at: https://issuu.com/reset-magazine/docs/calm-record-of-the-year-1718 (accessed: 29th August 2019).

Campaign for Living Miserably (CALM (2019) *About CALM: FAQ*. Available at: https://thecalmzone.net/about-calm/faq/ (accessed: 29th August 2019).

Cheung, R. (2018) *International Comparisons of Health and Wellbeing in Early Childhood*. London: The Nuffield Trust. Available at: https://nuffieldtrust.org.uk/files/2018-03/1521031084_child-health-international-comparisons-report-web (accessed: 28th August 2019df).

Children & Young People's Mental Health Coalition (2019) *Mental Health of Men and Boys Inquiry: Women and Equalities Committee*. Available at: http://data.parliament.uk/writtenevidence/committeeevidence.svc/evidencedocument/women-and-equalities-committee/mental-health-of-men-and-boys/written/103360.html (accessed: 29th August 2019).

The Children's Society (2019) *The Good Childhood Report: 2019 Summary*. Available at: https://childrenssociety.org.uk/sites/default/files/the_good_childhood_report_2019_summary.pdf (accessed: 29th August 2019).

Connell, R. (2005) *Masculinities* (2nd edn.). Cambridge: Polity Press.

Dean, M., Harwood, R. and Kasari, C. (2017) 'The art of camouflage: gender differences in the social behaviors of girls and boys with autism spectrum disorder', *Autism*, 21(6), pp. 678–689.

Department for Education (DfE) (2013) *Early Years Foundation Stage Profile Results in England, 2013*. Available at: https://assets.publishing.service.gov.uk/government/uploads/system/uploads/attachment_data/file/252223/SFR43_2013_Text.pdf (accessed: 29th August 2019).

Department for Education (DfE) (2018) *Early Years Foundation Stage Profile Results in England, 2018*. Available at: https://assets.publishing.service.gov.uk/government/uploads/system/uploads/attachment_data/file/748814/EYFSP_2018_Main_Text.pdf (accessed: 29th August 2019).

Early Education (2012) *Development Matters in the Early Years Foundation Stage (EYFS)*. Available at: https://foundationyears.org.uk/wp-content/uploads/2012/03/Development-Matters-FINAL-PRINT-AMENDED.pdf (accessed: 29th August 2019).

Farooq, M.A., Parkinson, K.N., Adamson, A.J., Pearce, M.S., Reilly, K., Hughes, A.R., Janssen, X., Basterfield, L. and Reilly, J.J. (2018) 'Timing of the decline in physical activity in childhood and adolescence: Gateshead Millennium Cohort Study', *British Journal of Sports Medicine*, 52(15), pp. 1002–1006.

Fausto-Sterling, A., Garcia Coll, C. and Lamare, M. (2012) 'Sexing the baby: Part 1 – What do we really know about sex differentiation in the first three years of life?', *Social Science & Medicine*, 74(11), pp. 1684–1692.

Gould, J. and Ashton-Smith, J. (2011) 'Missed diagnosis or misdiagnosis? Girls and women on the autism spectrum', *Good Autism Practice (GAP)*, 12(1), pp. 34–41.

Hamblin, E. and Young, H. (2017) *Gender-Sensitive Approaches to Addressing Children and Young People's Emotional and Mental Health and Well-being*. London: National Children's Bureau. Available at: https://ncb.org.uk/sites/default/files/field/attachment/NCB%20-%20Examples%20of%20gender-sensitive%20practice%20with%20CYP%20-%20Aug%202017.pdf (accessed: 28th August 2019).

Josephidou, J. (2017) *Perceptions of ECEC (Early Childhood Education and Care) Practitioners on How their Gender Influences their Approaches to Play*. PhD thesis. Lancaster University. Available at: https://eprints.lancs.ac.uk/id/eprint/125771/1/2018josephidouphd.pdf.pdf (accessed: 29th August 2019).

Loomes, R., Hull, L. and Mandy, W.P.L. (2017) 'What Is the male-to-female ratio in autism spectrum disorder? A systematic review and meta-analysis', *Journal of the American Academy of Child and Adolescent Psychiatry*, 56(6), pp. 466–474.

Mondschein, E.R., Adolph, K.E. and Tamis-LeMonda, C.S. (2000) 'Gender Bias in Mothers' Expectations about Infant Crawling', *Journal of Experimental Child Psychology*, 77, pp. 304–316.

nasen (2016) *Girls and Autism: Flying Under the Radar*. Staffordshire: Nasen. Available at: https://nasen.org.uk/resource/flying-under-the-radar-pdf.html (accessed: 28th August 2019).

National Autistic Society (2018) *Gender and Autism*. Available at: https://autism.org.uk/about/what-is/gender.aspx (accessed: 29th August 2019).

NHS (2018a) *Mental Health of Children and Young People in England, 2017*. Available at: https://files.digital.nhs.uk/F6/A5706C/MHCYP%202017%20Summary.pdf (accessed: 29th August 2019).

NHS (2018b) *Mindfulness*. Available at: www.nhs.uk/conditions/stress-anxiety-depression/mindfulness/ (accessed: 29th August 2019).

Plan International (2016) *Gender Inequality and Early Childhood Development*. Available at: https://plan-international.org/publication/2017-06-08-gender-inequality-and-early-childhood-development#download-options (accessed: 29th August 2019).

RCPCH (Royal College of Paediatrics and Child Health) (2013) *UK-WHO Growth Charts - 0-4 Years*. Available at: https://rcpch.ac.uk/resources/uk-who-growth-charts-0-4-years (accessed: 28th August 2019).

RCPCH (Royal College of Paediatrics and Child Health) (2017) *State of Child Health: Report 2017*. Available at: https://rcpch.ac.uk/sites/default/files/2018-09/soch_2017_uk_web_updated_11.09.18.pdf (accessed: 29th August 2019).

Sidebotham, P., Fraser, J., Covington, T., Freemantle, J., Petrou, S., Pulikottil-Jacob, R., Cutler, T. and Ellis, C. (2014) 'Understanding Why Children Die in High-Income Countries', *The Lancet*, 384 (9946), pp. 915–927.

Sport England (2018) *Active Lives Children and Young People Survey: Academic Year 2017/18*. Available at: https://sportengland.org/media/13698/active-lives-children-survey-academic-year-17-18.pdf (accessed: 29th August 2019).

Unicef (2011) *Boys and Girls in the Life Cycle: Sex-disaggregated Data on a Selection of Well-being Indicators, from Early Childhood to Young Adulthood*. New York: United Nations Children's Fund. Available at: https://unicef.org/media/files/Gender_hi_res.pdf (accessed: 28th August 2019).

Unicef (2017) *Gender Equality: Glossary of Terms and Concepts*. Available at: www.unicef.org/rosa/media/1761/file/Gender%20glossary%20of%20terms%20and%20concepts%20.pdf (accessed: 21st November 2019).

Webb, R. (2017) *How Not to be a Boy*. Edinburgh: Canongate Books Ltd.

WHO Multicentre Growth Reference Study Group (2006) 'Assessment of sex differences and heterogeneity in motor milestone attainment among populations in the WHO Multicentre Growth Reference Study', *Acta Paediatrica*, 450, pp. 66–75.

Wolfe, I., Macfarlane, A., Donkin, A., Marmot, M. and Viner, R. (2014) *Why Children Die: Death in Infants, Children and Young People in the UK Part A*. Available at: https://ncb.org.uk/sites/default/files/uploads/documents/Policy_docs/why_children_die_full_report.pdf (accessed: 29th August 2019).

Women and Equalities Committee (2018) *Mental Health of Men and Boys: Inquiry Launched*. Available at: https://parliament.uk/business/committees/committees-a-z/commons-select/women-and-equalities-committee/news-parliament-2017/mental-health-men-boys-launch-17-19/ (accessed: 29th August 2019).

Women and Equalities Committee (2019) *Oral evidence: Mental health of men and boys, HC 1721*. Available at: http://data.parliament.uk/writtenevidence/committeeevidence.svc/evidencedocument/women-and-equalities-committee/mental-health-of-men-and-boys/oral/103829.html (accessed: 29th August 2019).

World Health Organisation (2016) *Growing up unequal: gender and socioeconomic differences in young people's health and well-being*. Available at: http://euro.who.int/__data/assets/pdf_file/0003/303438/HSBC-No.7-Growing-up-unequal-Full-Report.pdf?ua=1 (accessed: 29th August 2019).

World Health Organisation (2018) *A child under 15 dies every 5 seconds around the world*. Available at: https://who.int/news-room/detail/18-09-2018-a-child-under-15-dies-every-5-seconds-around-the-world- (accessed: 28th August 2019).

PART IV

Conclusion

CHAPTER

Ways forward

How can we disrupt gendered scripts in the Early Years?

Introduction

Now we are nearing the end of our discussion about gender issues in the Early Years, think back to some of the ideas we considered in Chapter 1 (Introduction: Still talking about gender?). Do you remember that we pondered the idea of whether it was still pertinent to be talking about gender in 2020? A quick rummage through online media reveals: women being asked to cover up if breastfeeding on an aeroplane, men convicted of killing their female partner claiming it was a sex game gone wrong, what to do if you are being financially abused by a partner and similar stories. All these headlines offer a strong indication that patriarchy (systems and structures that reinforce gender inequalities) is alive and kicking – along with all its negative impacts. Jenna Karvunidis, who is noted as being the 'inventor' of the gender-reveal party (we hasten to add this is not a political party but one where friends and family are invited to witness parents-to-be discovering the sex/gender of their imminent baby), indicates that she wishes she had never started the whole thing as she can see how it 'saddles ... [the] kid with a whole identity' (Ho, 2019). Therefore, we hope we have convinced you not just to keep thinking about gender, but also to *actively* think about gender. What do we mean by *actively*? Well in this context we believe this means to think about how, whether as an individual or part of a team, you can challenge and disrupt some of the key scripts surrounding gender in the Early Years at either a micro level, a macro level or both. Therefore, this chapter will draw together all of the ideas and discussions we have considered throughout the book, whether they concern gender issues for young children, the early years workforce or wider society. As we propose some possible ways forward to consider, we will:

- help you develop your understanding of what it means to critically reflect on gender issues in the Early Years,

Conclusion

- explore opportunities practitioners can take to disrupt the gendered discourses and practices being used by children, parents and colleagues daily,
- highlight the positive impact that GST (gender sensitivity training) could have on the early years workforce and considering what this might look like in practice.

At the same time, we will turn the spotlight on ourselves, challenging each other to consider any stereotypical thinking we may hold about gender (Hogan, 2012). We will consider where these stereotypes might have emerged from and how they are reinforced. We will also draw on up-to-date research (Warin, 2017) to think about what the implications are for young children and for practice if those who work in early years settings are encouraged to 'disrupt' (Butler, 1990) gendered discourses and scripts.

What does critically reflecting on gender issues really mean?

It's easy to throw words like 'critical' and 'reflect' around but much harder to pin these words down and find a shared understanding which will help us move early years practice forward, particularly in terms of issues around gender. However, being able to critically reflect is a key part of being an effective practitioner in an effective workforce (Urban et al., 2012).

The importance of criticality

If you are a student, your tutors will often ask you to adopt a critical stance or write on your essays: 'Try to be more critical'. Many students find this difficult in their written work but here we are challenging you to develop this approach in your practice in the ECEC setting. We are not asking you to criticise your colleagues or the parents that you work with, however, we are asking you to adopt a questioning approach and not shy away from raising problematic issues or having difficult conversations. For example, read the case study below and decide how you could respond to Mimi to open up a critical discussion.

Case study

Mimi is on teaching practice as part of her EYTS training. You are working in the parallel reception class. Over coffee in the staff room you ask her how it is going. She responds that she is really enjoying working with the children and feels she is doing well. However, she then adds that she is relieved that she has not been placed in the parallel reception class because it is 'boy-heavy' and therefore must be a very difficult class to teach.

How could you respond to Mimi to support her engaging in more critical thinking about gender? Remember that you don't want to patronise or position yourself as the 'expert' who is going to reveal to Mimi the error of her ways as far as her understanding of gender is concerned (Hogan, 2012); rather, you want to ask questions which will enable an 'open and critical discussion on the topic of gender' (Hogan, 2012, p. 1). Make a list of three key questions you could ask before you look at our suggestions.

Suggested questions

1. I agree with you that there is certainly a stereotype around the difficulties of boy-heavy classes. What have you noticed the difficulties are? (In this way you have introduced the term 'stereotype', which might lead her to believe that not everyone holds this point of view. Then by asking her about her own experiences she is having to question what she has actually observed through the lens of the term 'stereotype'.)

2. Do you think we can do anything as adults to address these suggested differences? (In this way you are asking her to look at her own behaviours and practices (and perhaps those of her colleagues) and also not to regard the children (here boys) in a deficit way. You could be signposting how she could begin to disrupt assumptions about gender.)

3. Do you think there are approaches to teaching and classroom management that would be supportive of children regardless of gender? (In this way you are encouraging her to think beyond gender binaries in essentialist ways but to consider gender-neutral practices that all children could benefit from.)

All of this ability to reflect on practice links to the key idea of the reflective practitioner – a key disposition for all who work with young children.

Reflecting and reflection

Just as we reflect on children's learning as practitioners, we also need to be able to reflect on gender in the workplace and the practices, behaviours and scripts we see used. Connell, the eminent sociologist who we have cited throughout this book, wrote a recent blog post which described how she had recently made a cup of tea. As she picked up the carton of milk, she realised she was shaking it for no reason. Having reflected on why she had done this she remembered that growing up she had had to do this to make sure that any cream was evenly distributed. In this way, it was almost as if her arm had become 'socialised' to this action. Do you think that we too, in the early years setting, engage in unnecessary practices without thinking about whether they are really necessary?

Those who work with young children are constantly told to reflect on their practice, but this can sometimes be difficult to do. We always like to refer back to the 'What? So what? Now what?' questions; for example, if we see a practice that we feel reinforces gender differences in a negative way we need to ask ourselves:

- What exactly is happening? Can we describe it factually?
- How are the children reacting?
- What could the implications of this practice be?
- How can I intervene in a positive way?
- What is the best way to 'disrupt' what I see or hear?
- Is there a better way to do x/y/z?

If practitioners feel confident asking questions about their own practice then they can encourage the children to ask, challenge and enhance practice also. When this kind of reflection occurs it is not just the 'conforming reflection' we carry out, that Caroline Jones argues we do because we know we are supposed to, but rather it is 'transforming reflection' which 'suggest[s]fundamental change, and … promote[s] equity' (Jones, 2014, p. 359).

A 'competent systems' model

By constantly keeping these two key words at the heart of our practice we are contributing to what Urban et al. (2012) would call a competent system for ECEC. However, accountability in this system does not lie with the individual practitioner – for example in this context to disrupt harmful gender scripts – but rather it is about the practitioner being supported and encouraged to do this by the layers of context s/he is working within.

From research carried out by Urban et al. (2011) in the then 27 member states of the EU (and one candidate state, Croatia) ideas around quality in ECEC were identified. One key idea that was returned to again and again in the report informed by this research was the need for practitioners to be critically reflective and at the same time to be supported in this criticality. For example, they cite that reflection must happen at the four different levels of:

- the individual,
- the institution and team,
- inter-institution,
- governance (p. 33).

So, we could argue that thinking actively about gender should be happening at these four different levels.

Urban et al. (2012) assert that new ways of thinking about professionalism in ECEC are needed. They suggest a competency model based on a reflection on values and the importance of provision for continuing professional development

(CPD). They cite Vandenbroeck et al. (2010) who describe the practitioner as one who should always ask: 'do I do the right things rather than "Am I doing this right?"'

Sharmahd et al. (2018) emphasise a move away from the lone reflective practitioner to develop the idea of reflecting in groups. For example, they too suggest that time should be set aside for professional development when practitioners are not surrounded by children and where they can reflect on individual cases of pedagogy and practice. They link their rationale for this to Peeters et al.'s findings (2015) that 'long-term continuing professional development (CPD) interventions integrated into practice, such as pedagogical guidance and coaching in reflection groups, have been proved effective in very different contexts' (pp. 57–58).

What is gender sensitivity training and what could its impact be?

Defining GST

The term 'gender sensitivity training' is one that has been used by some researchers who focus on the gender imbalance of the early years workforce (Warin, 2015). Some suggest that such training would be a good way forward in terms of addressing this imbalance and other issues arising from it. However, what does this term really mean and what would this kind of training look like in practice? Robinson and Jones Diaz (2006) talk about practitioner reflexivity when considering gender implications in early childhood. Warin (2015) suggests 'the training of gender sensitivity' (p. 103) explicitly, highlighting how it must 'become a key element of initial teacher training (ITT) and continuing professional development (CPD) if we want to disrupt the slow but steady progress of gender entrenchment' (ibid.). She challenges her reader by asking 'How can we train male and female pre-school staff to model gender-flexible behaviours in front of their child and parent audience?' (ibid.). Hogan (2012) describes teaching strategies with early childhood students which allow 'spaces for honest, open and critical discussion on the topic of gender' (p. 1).

We would argue that all those who work with young children and their families need such opportunities to explore gender in a critical way, whether through CPD provision or university courses. However this training was given, participants would be able to examine their own and others' assumptions about how gender is performed; in so doing, they would take their own life experiences as a starting point. In this way, an understanding of the implications of gender construction, and how this can be problematic, would be developed.

By firstly being given the opportunity to look at gender more widely in a holistic way, we are then able to consider ideas and understandings about what this means for us as practitioners who work with young children on a day-to-day basis. For example, by considering examples of women complaining on social media about being catcalled, we can reflect on whether this has been part of our own experience and, if so, what the implications are. We then need to consider how these implications relate to the world of ECEC by drawing, for example, on the Zero Tolerance (2013) resources which make direct links between gender equalities in ECEC and gender inequalities among adults –we spoke about these back in Chapter 2 (Does a child's gender impact on how they play?). Once we have examined links to our own practice in this way we can then begin to consider how we might potentially lead on the practice of others, both in the workplace and in our interactions with parents.

Being able to lead on gender sensitivity in the workplace should be a non-negotiable outcome for participants in GST; it would not suffice for us to merely be able to ponder over our own practices. If GST is to have any impact at all, those who have attended it would need to feel empowered, equipped and energised to impact on the practice of others through their ability to challenge and disrupt gender (Butler, 1990) and question normalised discourses (Hogan, 2012; Robinson and Jones Diaz, 2006). It is necessary to recognise here that a willingness to lead on gender sensitivity in the ECEC setting would not be a straightforward undertaking for these participants; we have signposted many times in this book the problematic nature of discussing gender. People can feel attacked, become confrontational and adopt both contradictory (Robinson and Jones Diaz, 2006) and essentialist scripts (Ashely, 2003) or demonstrate a commitment to upholding patriarchal gender norms (Connell and Pearse, 2015). Because of all these inherent tensions, we would advise against providing training which consists of one-off sessions. Rather we would advocate for an approach which allows for progression of ideas over a period of time where participants would have the support of either online or face to face groups. In this way those who felt the weight of responsibility and the need to take action to tackle gender inequalities in their ECEC workplace would feel they were not a lone voice. This support could mirror MacNaughton's curriculum clubs (2005), which offered practitioners a designated time and space to unpick and explore the power issues potentially happening within their own pedagogy and practice. If GST was embedded in this way – a 'drip drip' approach rather than one-off input with no follow-up support – it is clear that it has potential for disrupting gender (Butler, 1990).

Therefore, it is possible that GST can impact at three different levels. Firstly, it could support individual practitioners in examining gender critically in a holistic way. This in turn could, secondly, lead them onto examining their own practices in the workplace and, thirdly, empower them to both lead on gender-equal pedagogies and challenge and disrupt gendered behaviours and practices. In this way they would be considering gender in various places on Connell's continuum (2016) for thinking and talking about gender, such as their individual interactions and everyday issues of 'relationships, [and] personal identities' (p. 4) at one end and then further wider implications at the other. If this potential is realised, then the importance of GST is apparent.

The importance of GST

Therefore, we argue – as we begin to conclude this journey into gender – that the type of training that GST could provide is important because of the opportunities it will give practitioners to question everyday assumptions. By interrogating assumed practices and behaviours, those who participate in the training have the potential to shift from a gender-blind stance to one that is sensitive to gendered constructions. This sensitivity would require participants to make decisions, going forward, about when it was necessary and appropriate to disrupt the gendered scripts they see being used around them in the workplace.

One of the reasons that GST could be so important is that it would give practitioners the opportunity, seldom afforded in their daily routines, to question their own and others' beliefs about gender. Often, ECEC practitioners are handed down both practices and scripts which they are then never given the opportunity to question or indeed they are not listened to if they try to do so (Brownhill and Oates, 2016). In this way, gender scripts in the ECEC setting may have become normalised over time.

A movement from 'gender blindness to gender consciousness' (Warin and Adriany, 2017, p. 384) on the part of participants would be a key outcome for those engaging in GST. In practice this would mean an ability to engage at a deeper, more reflective level, in discussions around gender both in the workplace and in the wider world. Through this reflection practitioners would bring a new dimension to their work, perhaps a dimension they had not considered before. In so doing they would be enabled to meet the benchmark standards for ECS, which require those in the children's workforce to challenge gender in ECEC (QAA, 2014, p. 5). This challenge would come about by the way they were subsequently equipped to disrupt both gendered scripts and gendered practices.

There are a variety of ways that GST could prepare them to disrupt gendered practices. One of these could be, for example, that they would have increased confidence to question and speak out about what they see. They would acquire both a new terminology and a louder voice as ECEC practitioners to position themselves, not as a workforce that has things 'done to them' (Brownhill and Oates, 2016), but rather as a workforce with agency.

Therefore, GST is important because it could provide practitioners with the tools to be able to think and act in different ways that run counter to the 'normalising' (Hogan, 2012) narratives of gender and also empower them to be agents of change. As suggested above, one of the tools might be a new vocabulary to challenge and disrupt gender, or examples and strategies they can draw on in their daily practices. Through exploration of their daily practices in the workplace, practitioners could be enabled to have a voice on these key issues so that the gender sensitivity of the workforce is something that they have control over rather than something done to them. The following section will set out specifically what GST could look like in practice, drawing on some work already undertaken in this area.

Conclusion

TABLE 11.1 Getting your audience to think about gender

Provocation	Example
Music video	'Stupid Girls' by Pink
Newspaper headline	'Never mind Brexit, who won Legs-it?' (Daily Mail, March 28, 2017)
TV programme	Friends: 'The one with the male nanny'
Social media	#dearcatcallers

Strategies for GST

A GST session would look very different depending on whether it was part of a university teaching session, a CPD twilight session or even part of a staff meeting in an early years setting. We are certainly not about to set out here exactly how it *should* be done; rather, we are going to make some suggestions about how it *could* be done, offering some illustrations of things that have worked successfully (or not!) in the past. One strength we have, as those who work with young children, is the power of the 'provocation'; we have found this to be true with adults as much as with children. Therefore, to initiate a session, we suggest a great idea to introduce participants would be some kind of stimulus that would provoke their thoughts about gender in a non-threatening way. Table 11.1 shares some ideas.

We are sure you can think of many more; as you can see, the stimulus does not necessarily have to be about the world of ECEC; rather it is a provocation which could act as a prompt for thinking about gender at a macro level. Participants would then be asked to talk generally about their response to the stimulus. Their thinking would be scaffolded by guided questions, some of which would encourage them to consider whether any of the content aligned with their own experiences or observations. Using a stimulus to prompt learning is a key part of ECEC pedagogy, so it is a teaching and learning device with which participants should be familiar in their daily work. This also aligns with Hogan's (2012) focus on encouraging her students to use their own life stories as a starting point to explore gender. At this point in the training participants are looking at particular gender issues through either the lens of their own experience or, potentially, the lens of their co-participants' experiences that have been vocalised to the group. It is at this stage in the training that an additional lens (or lenses) needs to be introduced to extend their critical thinking further.

The lens that needs to be presented at this stage is a theoretical one to help us understand further how gender might be played out in society. For example, in training already delivered, participants have been given a brief overview of some of the key ideas and concepts by such theorists as Anderson (2012), Butler (1990), Connell (2005), or Crenshaw (1991) and have been asked to reflect on them. An important consideration is how these, at times, quite complex ideas can be made accessible for a diverse audience without 'dumbing down' (Haggis, 2007) or misrepresenting the theorists' ideas in any way. Some of these writers facilitate an inclusive approach because they have made a conscious decision, such as Anderson (2012), to write in an accessible way. Others, such as Connell (2005), supplement their more academic writing with social media blogs which enable them to reach a diverse audience; this has proved to be effective material to use with both students and practitioners. Others like Butler (1990), whose use of written language may act as a barrier to students' understanding, have also recorded useful videos. Butler explains her key ideas in a less gatekeeping manner and in a way that students have already found valuable. With some, such as Crenshaw (1991), it has often been more helpful to look at, rather than the original sources, other sources where they have been interviewed about their ideas. At the same time, participants will have mixed academic levels and so there will be a need for differentiation and signposting so that those who are inclined to follow up key ideas and go back to original sources are clear on how to do this.

It is also important to present participants with a variety of theorists and thinkers at one time, so that they can choose the idea that resonates with them best rather than feeling that they are being preached at or dictated to (Hogan, 2012). Once they have been introduced to these lenses then we would return to look at the stimulus through the lens of their own choosing. At this point they are already beginning to look at gendered behaviours and practices in a different way. If the training stops at this point, then they are possibly thinking about gender in a macro way so they now need to be encouraged to ask the important 'So what?' question and relate these ideas to the work they do with children.

The proceeding step would then be for participants to make links to their own practice. If, for example, they had re-examined a music video in the light of their chosen theoretical lens, they would then need to ascertain if there were any links to ECEC in three ways. Firstly, they would need to consider if they recognised any of these gendered behaviours in the world of ECEC generally; secondly, if these same gendered behaviours were prevalent in their own ECEC setting; and thirdly, whether they had ever disrupted this gendered script in any way. It is at this point, it could be argued, that they start to become empowered because they can begin to realise their own potential and agency in initiating change. Furthermore, because the teaching and learning strategy around this part of the training would focus on group discussion and therefore co-construction of ideas, the participants would also be equipping themselves with tools and strategies to take back to the workplace. This approach has been successfully carried out in GST sessions already; for example, participants considered one particular recent music video ('Feels' by Calvin Harris) which featured four famous musicians: one female and three male. When the students first watched the video, they focused more on the lyrics of the song and found it difficult to describe how the four musicians might be positioning themselves in gendered ways. However, on a subsequent viewing, having considered some of the theories mentioned above, they began to talk in terms of 'emphasised femininity' (Connell, 1987) to describe the female musician who was the only one of the four to be in a supine position and was continually pulling up her skirt to reveal her thigh; 'hegemonic' (Connell, 2005) to describe one whose body language emphasised both leadership and aggression; and 'inclusive masculinity' (Anderson, 2012) to describe both the clothing and way of moving of another.

The final element of the training, designed to support the participants in making even tighter links between the session content and ECEC, is to provide them with a case study, as we have done throughout this book, based on real or hypothetical situations. They are encouraged to document their own personal response to the case study, linking this response to both their own personal philosophy, informed by their sense of values and any theoretical lenses discussed in the session. Time to document their ideas would be followed by a 'group think' about the case study. It is at this point that the person leading the session is able to carry out an informal assessment of any development of ideas that has taken place. This informal assessment also provides useful formative information which can be used to plan the following session; for example, it can reveal misconceptions, assumptions and rigid scripts that participants are more reluctant to give up.

By adopting pedagogies that practitioners would be familiar and comfortable with, providing an appropriate theoretical lens as an underpinning tool, and then supporting the participants in making clear links between group discussions and their own practice, participants could effectively examine gender critically within the context of ECEC. At the same time, it is necessary to be mindful of the different 'institutional biographies', a term Britzman (1986) uses to describe the cultural baggage brought by student teachers into the classroom. Tutor awareness of this 'baggage' would support a possible understanding of participants' scripts, values and behaviours and therefore allow for an adaption of both content and delivery to best suit the learning needs of the particular audience.

A reflection on training already carried out reveals that contradictory discourses (Anderson, 2012; Sumsion, 2000) are a key feature of audience participation. This phenomenon suggests that long-term, ongoing input could be more effective than one-off training presentations. In this way, participants could continually return to key ideas and therefore be supported more effectively in exploring how their own gender has been constructed or how they may have been socialised into behaving in certain gendered ways. Once able to discuss this construction critically they could then proceed to explore how their socialisation may impact in turn on the way that they socialise the children they work with.

Without the introduction of GST, it could be suggested that initiatives to recruit more men into ECEC, as we discussed in Chapter 7 (How can we achieve a more gender balanced workforce?) may be misplaced. Simply looking to recruit more men, even if successful, will have little impact on wider societal gender issues if practitioners continue to draw on prescribed gender scripts because they have never had the opportunities to challenge or question them. Rather, the emphasis should move to one that looks for the missing behaviours, such as gender flexibility (Warin, 2017) and an ability to 'critique gender' (Hogan, 2012). In this way, the focus would move away from practitioner gender and turn towards practitioner skills and dispositions. This shift of focus would mean a downplaying of the 'missing men' (Thornton and Bricheno, 2006) argument and an emphasis on a 'missing pedagogy' argument. The focus would be more on recruiting a diverse workforce with diverse skills who can be gender-flexible and not have to rely on their personality or their gender to inform the best practice. These would be practitioners who construct themselves in the ECEC workplace 'by choices that transcend given circumstances' (Connell, 1987, p. 211) such as the cultural scripts that have been handed down to them because of their gender.

Final reflection

And so our journey of exploring gender comes to an end – for the moment. After pausing for breath, you will have to consider how as a student, practitioner, or an advocate for children, you will continue the journey and take responsibility for disrupting those discourses and practices that have become taken for granted and yet continue to reinforce gender stereotypes that impact negatively on outcomes for children, the early years workforce and society as a whole. Remember Connell's thoughts that we added to a continuum for thinking and talking about gender in Chapter 1. In your everyday life you can do little about global issues at the far right-hand end of the line – you can do little about femicide and militarisation. However, you do have complete control over everyday issues of 'intimate relationships, [and] personal identities' (Connell, 2016, p. 4). You do have agency in how you interact with children, their parents and your colleagues. By exploring your own gendered construction, you can recognise that what happens at one end of the 'gender thinking continuum' can impact on what happens at the other. You can consider how flexible you are able to be in your professional behaviours by considering how your gender influences how you interact with young children and if there are contradictions in the discourses and behaviours you use. You can consider how you can take time and space with your colleagues and peers to critically reflect on gender issues in Early Years so that everyone can develop their practice into one that is both gender-flexible (Warin and Adriany, 2017) and also highly effective for young children.

Key points

- If we work with young children and their families, it is important we take the time to reflect critically, not just on children's learning and development, but any issues which could be linked to gender.

- As we engage in this critical reflection, we need to look for opportunities to challenge ourselves in our practices and also encourage our colleagues to challenge themselves also.
- This challenging of practices can be formalised into a form of CPD (continuing professional development) called gender sensitivity training.

Further reading

https://contemplatingchildhoods.com

This is our weekly blog where we critically reflect on many issues linked to early childhood including gender issues. We would love you to join us!

References

Anderson, E. (2012) *Inclusive Masculinity: The Changing Nature of Masculinities*. Oxon: Routledge.

Ashley, M. (2003). Primary schoolboys' identity formation and the male role model: An exploration of sexual identity and gender identity in the UK through attachment theory, *Sex Education*, 3(3), pp. 257–270.

Britzman, D.P. (1986). Cultural myths in the making of a teacher: biography and social structure in teacher education, *Harvard Educational Review*, 56(4), pp. 442–456.

Brownhill, S. and Oates, R. (2016) 'Who do you want me to be? An exploration of female and male perceptions of 'imposed' gender roles in the early years', *Education 3–13*, 45(5), pp. 658–670.

Butler, J. (1990) *Gender Trouble: Feminism and the Subversion of Identity*. London: Routledge.

Connell, R.W. (1987). *Gender and Power*. Cambridge: Polity Press.

Connell, R. (2005) *Masculinities*. 2nd. Cambridge: Polity Press.

Connell, R. and Pearse, R. (2015). *Gender: In World Perspective (Polity Short Introductions)*, 3rd edn. Cambridge: Polity Press.

Connell, R. (2016) '100 Million Kalashnikovs: Gendered power on a world scale', *Debate Feminista*, 51, pp. 3–17.

Crenshaw, K. (1991) 'Mapping the margins: Intersectionality, identity, and violence against women of color', *Stanford Law Review*, 43(6), pp. 1241–1300.

Haggis, T. (2007) 'Pedagogies for diversity: Retaining critical challenge amidst fears of "dumbing down"', *Studies in Higher Education*, 31(5), pp. 521–535.

Ho, V. (2019) *Pioneer of gender-reveal party regrets sparking trend: 'Let kids be who they are'*. Available at: www.theguardian.com/culture/2019/jul/26/gender-reveal-party-pioneer-regrets-trend (accessed 27 July 2019).

Hogan, V. (2012). *Locating my teaching of gender in early childhood education teacher education within the wider discourse of feminist pedagogy and poststructuralist theory*. Paper presented at the Joint AARE/ APERA, Sydney. Available at; http://files.eric.ed.gov/fulltext/ED542504.pdf (accessed 23 July 2018).

Jones, C. (2014) Reflective practice, in: T. Waller and G. Davis (eds) *An Introduction to Early Childhood*, 3rd edn. London: Sage.

Peeters, J., Rohrmann, T. and Emilsen, K. (2015) 'Gender balance in ECEC: why is there so little progress?' *European Early Childhood Education Research Journal*, 23(3), pp. 302–314, doi: 10.1080/1350293X.2015.1043805.

QAA (Quality Assurance Agency) (2014) *Subject benchmark statement: Early childhood studies*. Available at: www.qaa.ac.uk/en/Publications/Documents/SBS-early-childhood-studies-14.pdf (accessed: 22nd August 2019).

Robinson, K.H. and Jones Diaz, C. (2006) *Diversity and Difference in Childhood: Issues for Theory and Practice*. London: Open University Press.

Sumsion, J. (2000). Negotiating otherness: A male early childhood educator's gender positioning, *International Journal of Early Years Education*, 8(2), pp. 129–140.

MacNaughton, G. (2005) *Doing Foucault in Early Childhood Studies*. Oxon: Routledge.

Thornton, M. and Bricheno, P. (2006). *Missing men in Education*. Stoke on Trent: Trentham Books.

Sharmahd, N., Peeters, J. and Bushati, M. (2018) 'Towards continuous professional development: Experiencing group reflection to analyse practice', *Eur Journal Education*, 53, pp. 58–65.

Urban, M., Vandenbroeck, M., Van Laere, K., Lazzari, A.&. and Peeters, J. (2011) *Competence Requirements in Early Childhood Education and Care: Final Report*. Brussels, Belgium: European Commission.

Urban, M., Vandenbroeck, M., Van Laere, K., Lazzari, A. and Peeters, J. (2012) 'Towards competent systems in early childhood education and care. implications for policy and practice', *European Journal of Education*, 47(4), pp. 508–526.

Vandenbroeck, M., Coussee, F. and Bradt, L. (2010) 'The social and political construction of early childhood education', *British Journal of Educational Studies*, 58, pp. 139–153.

Warin, J. (2015). 'Pioneers, professionals, playmates, protectors, 'poofs' and 'paedos': Swedish male pre-school teachers' construction of their identities', in: S. Brownhill, J. Warin and I. Wernersson (eds) *Men, Masculinities and Teaching in Early Childhood Education: International Perspectives on Gender and Care*. Oxon: Routledge.

Warin, J. (2017). Conceptualising the value of male practitioners in early childhood education and care: gender balance or gender flexibility, *Gender and Education*, doi:10.1080/09540253.2017.1380172

Warin, J. and Adriany, V. (2017) 'Gender flexible pedagogy in early childhood education', *Journal of Gender Studies*, 26(4), pp. 375–386.

Zero Tolerance (2013). *Just Like a Child: Challenging Gender Stereotyping in the Early Years. A Guide for Childcare Professionals*. Available from: www.zerotolerance.org.uk/resources/Just-Like-a-Child.pdf (Accessed 21st Nov, 2019).

Index

Note: References in *italics* are to figures, those in **bold** to tables.:

A-level choices 55
academic achievements 125
achievement 46–47; boys 47–49, 53; case study 56; Early Learning Goals 51–53; issues 49–51, **51**; through the education system 53–55
Adriany, V. 27, 28, 41, 159
age and gendered approaches to learning 38–40
agender, defined **3**
Aina, O.E. 25–26
Akande, A. 41
Albon, D. 5
Anderson, E. 39, 160, 161, 162
ASD (autistic spectrum disorder) 139–140, 141
asexual, defined **4**
Ashley, M. 2, 108
attachment theory 108
Australia: rough-and-tumble play 76
Austria: outdoor play 74

Barnes, S. 80
Baron-Cohen, S. 20, 24
behavioural disorders 140
Bem, S.L. 39
Bento, G. 74
Berentsen, J. 142, 143
Bernstein (1970) 38
bisexual, defined **4**
Bourdieu, P. 38
Bowlby, J. 126
boys: achievement 47–49, 53; learning 33–34, 35; mental health 139–142; physical health 135–137; at play 20–21, 23

Bradburn, E. 64
Bradbury, A. 36, 37–38, 51
Bretherton, I. *et al.* 76
Bricheno, P. 96, 107, 108, 163
British Household Panel Study 128
Britzman, D.P. 162
Brody, D. 3, 93, 97
Brooker, L. 38
Brownhill, S. 62–63, 97, 109, 126, 159
Bryan, N. 20
Burgess, A. 127
Burn, E. 6, 33, 50, 64, 65
Butler, J. 7, 160, 161

CACE (Central Advisory Council for Education) 63
CALM (Campaign Against Living Miserably) 144, 145
CALMzine 143, 144, 145
Cambule, L. 141
Cameron, C. 91
Cameron, P.A. 25–26
Campbell-Barr, V. *et al.* 110
Campbell, S.B. 124
career choices and learning 41–42
caring 105–106; caring for or caring about 107–109; case study 115–116; as female attribute 112, 115; and gender 111–114; passion of EY practitioners 109; and personality 111–112; professional love 108, 109–111, **111**; and social forces 112–114; theories 106–107
Carlson, S.M. 22

case studies 12; achievement 56; caring 115–116; critical reflection 154–155; fathers 129; gender and learning 42; gender-balanced workforce 97; gendered language 12–13; gendered play 28; gendered workforce 69–70, 83, **83**; health 145
Central Advisory Council for Education (CACE) 63
Centre for Social Justice 129
Cheung, R. 135
child-centred curriculum 27–28
Children and Young People's Mental Health Coalition (CYPMHC) 139
Children's Development and Workforce Council 63
Children's Society 134
cis-gender, defined **3**
Clarke, C. 121, 122, 125, 127, 128
Cohen, S. 46
Colley, H. 108, 109
Connell, R. 3, 9, 10, 13, 35, 143, **144**, 155, 158, 160, 161
Connell, R.W. 66, *66*, 67–68, 161–162, 163
continuing professional development (CPD) 157
Crenshaw, K. 36, 41, 160, 161
critical reflection 154; case study 154–155; competent systems model 156–157; reflecting and reflection 155–156
criticality 154
cultural baggage 162
cultural capital 38
culture and gendered approaches to learning 40–41
curriculum clubs 158
Cushman, P. 77–78, 91
CYPMHC (Children and Young People's Mental Health Coalition) 139

Dalli, C. 110
Davies, J. 88
Denmark: workforce gender 63
Department for Children, Schools and Families (DfCSF) 35
Department for Education (DfE) 35, 36, 54, 62–63, 88, 89, 126–127; SATS tests 49
Dias, G. 74

discipline 120–121
discourses **5**, 6, 32, 67–68
Dogra, N. 80–81

Eagly, A.H. 21
Early Education 12 95, 141
Early Learning Goals (ELGs) 51–53, 136
early years setting: child-centred curriculum 27–28; impact of 11; play 24–27
early years workforce 61; case study 69–70, 83, **83**; gender balance or imbalance? 4, 62–63; implications of gendered discourses 69; passion 109; practitioner skills and dispositions 96–97; reasons for gender imbalance 64–65; society's perceptions of men in *66*, 66–68; *see also* gender-balanced workforce; gender imbalance in early years workforce
Einarsdottir, J. 80
Eliassen, R. 93
Emilsen, K. 74, 75, 95
emotion **6**
emotional disorders 140, 141
English, L.M. 4
Equal Opportunities Commission 88
Equality Act (2010) 6
Eriksson, M. *et al.* 21
essentialist approach 2, 3, 8, 11, 13
European Commission Childcare Network 92
European Social Survey 128
European Union Labour Force Survey 128
EYFS (Early years foundation stage): Profile 36, 136, 142; Statutory Framework 26, 52, 105
Eysenck, H. 111
Eysenck Personality Questionnaire (EPQ) 112

Fagan, J. *et al.* 120–121
Farooq, M.A. *et al.* 136, 145
Farquhar, S. 109
'father figues' 126–127
fatherhood 119–120, 129
Fatherhood Institute 62, 67, 76–77, 88, 90, 124, 127, 128, 129
'fathering' 126, 127–128, 130
fathers **123**; case study 129; discipline 120–121; impact on child development 123–125, **125**; language 121–122; play 23, 122

Index

'feminisation of education' 36, 46, 50
feminism 4–5
Fletcher, R. *et al.* 23
football 35, 39
Foucault, M. 6, 32, 41–42, 67, 68
Framework of Masculinities 143–144, **144**
Freud, S. 112
Froebel, F. 64, 67

Garfield, C.F. 124
gay, defined **3**
GCSEs 54–55
GEAS *see* Global Early Adolescent Study
gender: binary approaches 6–7, **7**; children's understanding of 39; concept 2–3; definitions 2, **3–4**; at different levels 10–11; in early childhood context 8–11; impact of 1; labels **3–4**; theoretical lenses 4–6
gender-balanced workforce 87, 97–98; case study 97; need for 96–97; Norway 63, 69, 89, 93–94; practitioner skills and dispositions 96–97; Sweden 94–96; UK initiatives 88–92
gender blindness 142–143
gender equality: inequalities 51, **51**; young children and families 8–10
gender fluid, defined **3**
gender imbalance in early years workforce 73; 'androgynous professional practice' 78; case study 83, **83**; children's perspectives 79–82, **81**; cultural norms 82; 'gender flexibility' 79; gender-flexible practice 77–79; guided participation theory 82–83; 'holistic approach' 77–78; positive male influences? 74–77; reasons for 64–65
gender queer, defined **3**
gender schema theory 39
gender sensitivity training (GST) 157–158; importance of 159; strategies **160**, 160–163
gendered child 19–20
GenderEYE 88–89
genealogy 41–42
Georgeson, J. *et al.* 27
Gilligan, C. 106, 107
Girl Guiding Association 9
girls: language skills 21–22; mental health 139–142; physical health 136–139; at play 21–22, 23; school attendance 138

Girls' Attitude Survey 9, 25
Glenn, S.M. 22
Global Early Adolescent Study (GEAS) 40, 42
Goldman, R. 127, 128
Golombok, S. *et al.* 126, 127
Gray, B. 107
Greece: workforce gender 65
GST *see* gender sensitivity training
guided participation theory 82–83

H is for Harry (film) 38
Haggis, T. 161
Hamblin, E. 142, 143, 144
Harris, C. 161
Harris, K. 80
Harty, R. 80
health 134–135, 145–146; case study 145; hegemonic masculinities 143–145; mental health 134, 139–143; physical health 135–139; weight 134
Hedlin, M. *et al.* 94
hegemonic masculinities 143–145
heterosexual, defined **3**
Hilton, M. 64
Hirsh, P. 64
Hjalmarsson, M. 40
Ho, V. 153
Hogan Personality inventory 112
Hogan, V. 11, 157, 159, 160, 163
home learning environment (HLE) 37
homosexual, defined **3**
Hornslien, O. 93
Hungary: professional love 110
hyperactivity disorder 140

Indonesia: child-centred EY curriculum 40–41
initial teacher training (ITT) 157
institutional biographies 162
intersectionality 36, 41, 47, 53
intersexuality, defined **3**

Jaegera, M. 38
James, L. 113
Jarvis, P. 52
John, A. *et al.* 122, 124
Jones, A. 22
Jones, C. 156
Jones Diaz, C. 1–2, 4, 6, 7, 61, 67, 68, 157

Kaltvedt, E. 23
Karvunidis, J. 153
Kingdon, Z. 63
Knott, J. 54–55
Koch, B. 74, 75, 95, 109
Kohlberg, L. 39
Kollmayer, M. *et al.* 25
Kumar, S.S. 113–114

labels for sex and gender **3–4**
Lamb, C. 76
Lamb, M.E. 120–121, 122
Lancaster University 88
language 121–122; case study 12–13; girls 21–22; practitioner talk 25–26
learning 32–33, 42–43; boys 33–34, 35; and career choices 41–42; case study 42; gendered approaches 33–37, 38–41; gendered interests 33–34; gendered scripts 32; impact of age 38–40; impact of culture 40–41; literacy skills 36–37, 125; physical approaches 33–34; and social economic status 37–38
Lee, J. 108
lesbian, defined **3**
Lewicki, K. *et al.* 21
Lewis, M.E. 76
Lillehammer Model 94
Lindsey, E.W. *et al.* 124
literacy skills 36–37, 125
Lofdahl, A. 40
London Early Years Foundation (LEYF) 75, 89, 91
love, professional 108, 109–111, **111**
Lundetræ, K. 36
Lupton, B. 61
Lynch, M. 22

McBride, B.A. *et al.* 125
McBryde, C. *et al.* 52
McDonald, J.W. 35, 36
McLeod, J. 106
McMillan, M. 64, 67
MacNaughton, G. 23, 158
MacPhee, D. 113
Meland, A.T. 23
Men in Childcare charity 91–92

mental disorders in children 134, 139–140; gender-sensitive approaches 142–143, **143**; impact of hegemonic masculinities 143–145; rates of diagnoses 141–142
metanarratives **5**
Mikelson, K.S. 128
Millennium Cohort Study 136
mindfulness 142, 143
Mistry, M. 65, 67
MITEY (Men In The Early Years) 90–91
Modern Fatherhood 128
Mollegaard, S. 38
Mondschein, E.R. *et al.* 137
moral development theories 106
'moral panic' 46–50
Morgenroth, T. 7
Moss, G. 35, 36
Moss, P. 74, 95–96
motherhood 119–120, 129
'mothering' 126, 128, 130
mothers **123**; discipline 120–121; impact on child development 123–125, **125**; language 121–122; play 122
Moyles, J. 108, 109
Mukherji, P. 5

narratives 6
National Association of Special Educational Needs (nasen) 141
National child care strategy (1998) 62
National Curriculum 50
National Health Service (NHS) 139–140
National Literacy Trust 35
New Zealand: male early years practitioners 76–77, 93
Newland, L.A. *et al.* 123, 124
Noddings, N. 106–107
non-binary, defined **3**
Norway: Networks for Men in Kindergartens (MIB) 93; outdoor play 74–75; risky play 75; workforce gender 63, 69, 89, 93–94
nursery rhymes 114
nursing 107

Oates, R. 62–63, 97, 108, 126, 159
Oates, T. 50, 51
OECD 40, 48, 92, 94
Office for National Statistics 126

Index

Ofsted 19 48–49
O'Reilly, M. 80–81
O'Sullivan, J. 91
'othering' 2
outdoor play 74–77
Ouvry, M. 34
Owen, R. 64
Oxford English Dictionary 78, 119, 120

Paechter, C. 5–6, **5–6**
Page, J. 109–110
Pajares, F. 26
Pancsofar, L. 121–122
pansexual, defined **4**
passion 109
patriarchy 4, **5**, 66, 68
Paule, M. 35
Pearse, R. 3
peer competence 124–125
peer support 90
Peeters, J. *et al.* 63, 69, 93, 157
Pells, R. 46
Perkins, H. *et al.* 91
personality 111–112
physical approaches to learning 33–34
physical health outcomes for children 135; high-income countries 135–137; in the majority world 137–138
Piaget, J. 39
PISA (Programme for International Student Assessment) 36, 48, 53
Plan International 138–139
play 19–20, 28; boys 20–21, 23; case study 28; child-centred curriculum 27–28; early years setting 24–27; fantasy play 21–22; fathers 23, 122; further gender issues 22–24; gendered play 24–27; girls 21–22, 23; mothers 122; outdoor play 74–77; practitioner expectations 26–27; practitioner talk 25–26; risky play 75; rough-and-tumble play 22–23, 75–76, 122; superhero play 23
Plowden report (1967) 63
post-structural feminism 4
post-structuralism 5, **5–6**
power **5**, 24
practitioner talk 25–26
Pratt-Adams, S. 6, 33, 50, 64, 65

Pre-school Learning Alliance 65
Prendergast, S. 113
Price, D. 23
professional love 108, 109–111, **111**

queer theory 7

Raeburn, P. 122
reflection *see* critical reflection
regimes of truth 67
Rentzou, K. 65, 67
resistance **5**
Richards, J.R. 5, 13
Roberts-Holmes, G. 36, 37–38, 81
Robinson, K.H. 1–2, 4, 6, 7, 61, 67, 68, 157
Rogoff, B. 81–82
Rohrmann, T. 3
Rolfe, H. 88, 93
Ross and Taylor 1989 122
Routen, A.C. *et al.* 21
Royal College of Paediatrics and Child Health 137
Ryan, M.K. 7

Sandseter, E. 75
Sandström, M. *et al.* 26
SATs tests 54
Save the Children 48
schema 28, 39
school attendance 138
Scotland: Men in Childcare 91–92
scripts 6, 32, 67
self-efficacy 26–27
sex definitions and labels 3, **3–4**
sex role theory 9, 35, 143
Sharmahd, N. *et al.* 157
Sidebotham, P. *et al.* 137
single-sex schools 55
Skelton, C. 64
Smith, A. 46
social economic status (SES) and learning 37–38
social learning theory (SLT) 35, 39
Solheim, O.J. 36
Sood, K. 65, 67
Spain: children's health 135
Sport England 136
Stoet, G. 50

Sumsion, J. 76, 77, 78, 91
Sweden: children's health 135; Egalia 95–96; gender-balanced workforce 94–96; National Agency for Education 95; practitioner talk 26, 40

Tasker, F. 127
Tayler, K. 23
Taylor, M. 22
themes and objectives of the book 11–12
third gender, defined **3**
Thomson, R. *et al.* 128
Thornton, M. 96, 107, 108, 163
Tovey, H. 64
transgender, defined **3**
Turkey: workforce gender 63

UN Women 9
Understanding Society 128
Unicef 137–138, 142–143
Urban, M. *et al.* 156–157
Uttal, L. 109

Van Polanen, M. *et al.* 75, 122
Vandenbroeck, M. *et al.* 157
Vernon-Feagans, L. 121–122
Vine, S. 46
von Stauffenberg, C. 124
Vygotsky, L. 82

Warin, J. 77, 79, 90, 91, 92, 97, 127, 157, 159
Webb R. 144
weight 134
Whitebread, D. 52
Williams, R. 94
Winsler, A. *et al.* 120–121
Wohlegemuth, G. 97
Women and Equalities Committee 139, 141
Wood, W. 21
World Health Organisation 134, 136, 137; Multicentre Growth References Study Group 137
Wright, D. 88

Yogman, M. 124
Young, H. 142, 143, 144
Younger, M. *et al.* 35

Zero Tolerance 26–27, 158
zone of proximal development (ZPD) 82

For Product Safety Concerns and Information please contact our EU representative GPSR@taylorandfrancis.com
Taylor & Francis Verlag GmbH, Kaufingerstraße 24, 80331 München, Germany

www.ingramcontent.com/pod-product-compliance
Lightning Source LLC
Chambersburg PA
CBHW080736300426
44114CB00019B/2614